Management in the Built Environment in Ireland

MANAGEMENT IN THE BUILT ENVIRONMENT IN IRELAND

Margaret Linehan, Paul Greaney and Edel Foster

Gill Education
Hume Avenue
Park West
Dublin 12
www.gilleducation.ie

Gill Education is an imprint of M.H. Gill & Co.

© Margaret Linehan, Paul Greaney and Edel Foster 2010

978 07171 4801 1

Print origination in Ireland by O'K Graphic Design, Dublin
Printed by Sprintprint, Ireland

The paper used in this book is made from the wood pulp of managed forests. For every tree felled, at least one tree is planted, thereby renewing natural resources.

A CIP catalogue record for this book is available from the British Library.

CONTENTS

TABLES

FIGURES

1
INTRODUCTION TO MANAGEMENT

Learning outcomes

Following study of this chapter you will be able to:
- define management
- trace the historical development of management
- identify the main contributors to management theory
- understand the similarities and differences between various management perspectives.

1.1 Management defined

This chapter begins with an examination of what is meant by **management**. While there are many definitions of management, there is no universal agreement on what is meant by the term. From as early as 1903 management has been defined in various ways, for example, Taylor (1911):

> Knowing exactly what you want people to do, and then seeing that they do it in the best and cheapest way.

Taylor's definition, however, is rather simplistic, as management is a much more complex process. In 1916, Henri Fayol stated that:

> To manage is to forecast and plan, to organise, to command, to coordinate and to control.

Figure 1.1 Management activities

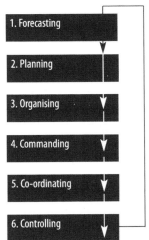

Fayol's definition of management therefore gives us six key elements (see Figure 1.1)

Fayol believed that *forecasting* and *planning* were concerned with looking at future activities in an organisation and drawing up plans of action to deal with situations that might arise. Forecasting and planning are fundamental aspects of construction management and are prerequisites for implementing a construction project.

Fayol viewed *organising* in terms of having the people and resources necessary to carry out organisational planning in a logical manner.

In the built environment, employees are one of the most important resources for all companies. The manner in which the available resources and skills are used is vital to providing what clients expect from their projects. Other resources include machinery that contractors have available to them and computer software packages that construction companies use, such as project management software (for example, Microsoft Project, Primavera, HorNET, etc.).

Fayol described *commanding* as 'maintaining activity among the personnel', that is, having a manager with a plan for a group of activities that have the same objective. Similarly, he viewed *co-ordinating* as a unifying activity, facilitating managers and employees to work together to achieve organisational goals. Finally, *controlling* meant that activities happen in accordance with the established policies and practices of an organisation.

Fayol's perspective viewed organisations from the top downwards, emphasising the hierarchical aspects of organisations. His definition has been criticised in the context of the flatter structures of modern organisations and of increased employee participation in decision-making processes.

Even though Fayol's study of management was conducted as long ago as the early 1900s, his management functions act as the core of management practice and study today, particularly for managing in the built environment.

Recent management theorists offer different definitions of management, such as Griffin (2008):

> Management is a set of activities (including planning and decision-making, organising, leading, and controlling) directed at an organisation's resources (human, financial, physical, and information) with the aim of achieving organisational goals in an efficient and effective manner.

It can be seen from Griffin's definition that the activities suggested by Fayol for understanding management are still incorporated into modern-day management theories. It is important, however, to note that Griffin's definition highlights *achieving organisational goals in an efficient and effective manner*. **Efficient** means using resources wisely and in a cost-effective way. Griffin defines **effective** as making the right decisions and implementing them successfully.

Reflecting the above, Naylor (2004) stated that:

> Management is the process of achieving organisational objectives, within a changing environment, by balancing efficiency, effectiveness and equity, obtaining the most from limited resources, and working with and through people.

Naylor's definition consists of five key terms:

1. **Achieving organisational objectives**—setting realistic targets or objectives and achieving them successfully.
2. **Within a changing environment**—organisations operate in a dynamic environment. Conditions in the built environment have changed significantly, for example projects are now more complex technically and contractually. Legislation concerning companies is more challenging; competition is stronger; and people's attitudes towards managers and work has changed. The environment consists of two major forces: the macro environment and the micro environment (see Chapter 2). *Macro-environmental factors* include:

   - the economic environment
   - technology
   - the political and legal environment
   - the social or cultural environment
   - the international environment.

   Micro-environmental factors consist of:

   - employees
   - investors
   - competitors
   - suppliers
   - distributors
   - customers.

3. **Balancing efficiency, effectiveness and equity**—combining the changing of inputs into outputs and achieving desired results while at the same time being fair to all employees.
4. **Obtaining the most from limited resources**—managers need to understand that they do not have unlimited resources and must therefore use the resources available to them as efficiently as possible.
5. **With and through other people**—having the right people at the right place at the right time to achieve organisational objectives.

1.2 Managing at different levels of the organisation

Organisations generally have three levels of management, represented by top managers, middle managers and first-line managers. **Top managers** make up the relatively small group of executives who manage the overall organisation. Titles found in this group include president, vice-president and chief executive officer (CEO). Top managers create the organisation's goals, overall strategy and operating policies.

Middle managers are primarily responsible for implementing the policies and plans developed by top managers and for supervising and co-ordinating the activities of lower-level managers.

First-line managers supervise and co-ordinate the activities of operating employees. First-line managers typically spend a large proportion of their time supervising the work of subordinates. A trade foreman is a first-line manager of the workers in his/her trade and is responsible for planning and controlling the work of the particular trade gang.

Managerial roles

Henry Mintzberg (a Canadian academic) closely observed the day-to-day activities of a group of CEOs by literally following them around and taking notes on what they did. From his observations, Mintzberg concluded that managers play ten different roles, as summarised in Table 1.1, and that these roles fall into three basic categories: interpersonal, informational, and decisional.

Table 1.1 Ten basic managerial roles

Category	Role	Sample Activities
INTERPERSONAL	Figurehead	Sod-turning on a new construction project.
	Leader	Encouraging the design team to be innovative in responding to the client's brief.
	Liaison	Co-ordinating design information between the architect, engineers and quantity surveyor.
INFORMATIONAL	Monitor	Scanning industry media for reports of prospective projects.
	Disseminator	Sending emails outlining new organisational opportunities.
	Spokesperson	Making a presentation to secure new work for the firm.
DECISIONAL	Entrepreneur	Developing new services for clients.
	Disturbance handler	Resolving conflict between members of the design team. Reviewing and balancing.
	Resource allocator	Achieving a workable compromise.
	Negotiator	

1.3 Management theories

The classical management perspective

The **classical management** perspective emerged during the late 1890s and early 1900s and consisted of two distinct areas:

1. *Scientific management* was concerned with the individual worker and issues such as the division of work, the establishment of authority and developing

solutions to problems of labour inefficiency.

2. *Classical organisation theory*, on the other hand, focused on managing the total organisation.

Early management theorists included Frederick Winslow Taylor in the United States, Henri Fayol in France and Max Weber in Germany.

Frederick Winslow Taylor

F. W. Taylor (1856–1915) was considered to be a pioneer in the scientific management field and he is often referred to as 'the father of scientific management'. His theories were based on his experience as a shop-floor worker and later as a manager.

Table 1.2 Taylor's principles of scientific management

Principle	Description
1. Observations	Making detailed timings with a stopwatch enabled Taylor to analyse each aspect of the production process. This method has been used in the built environment in establishing labour constants for construction activities.
2. Experiments	Taylor developed a science of work and devised experiments in order to achieve maximum efficiency.
3. Standardisation	From the data collected from observations and experiments, instructions were published which were to be followed by workers. Standardisation implied that managers had to ensure that workers were provided with the proper equipment and that this was used effectively. Statements used in the construction sector, particularly in relation to health and safety, are a development of Taylor's' standardisation.
4. Selection and Training	Taylor showed that output could be increased, with employees feeling less tired and earning up to 60% more pay as a result of the correct selection and training of personnel and the matching of staff to tasks.
5. Payment by Results	Taylor believed that workers were primarily motivated by pay. He experimented with differential piece-work plans which he believed would lead to increased prosperity for all. Piece-work systems were at the centre of scientific management. Piece-work contracts are used in the construction process, particularly for trade work such as brick/blocklaying, plastering and carpentry.
6. Co-operation	Management and workers were required to co-operate if everyone was to benefit from scientific management. Taylor, however, believed that the workers should remain under the control of their management and accept that management would be responsible for determining what was to be done and how the work was to be done.

At the beginning of the twentieth century many industrial plants were mechanised, yet the plants still employed thousands of staff to feed and unload the machines and materials. Business was expanding and capital was readily available, but labour was in short supply. The problem for management, therefore, was to organise the existing labour more efficiently. According to Gunnigle *et al.* (1999), this situation led to the emergence of modern management as a result of the need to plan, control, direct and organise the use of equipment, capital, materials and people in factories. During this time, working conditions were poor and workers could do little about this as they had little or no economic or political power.

Taylor observed that few, if any, workers put more than minimal effort into their daily work. He called this lack of effort *soldiering*, which he subdivided into *natural soldiering*, that is, workers' natural tendency to spare effort, and *systematic soldiering*, that is, the deliberate and organised restriction of work rate by employees. Taylor believed that soldiering was primarily a result of fear of unemployment. It was against this background that Taylor developed his ideas on management.

Taylor was primarily interested in the efficiency of working methods, and the solutions he devised were based on his own experience at work. He analysed each job by breaking it down into its component parts and then designed the quickest and best methods of operation for each part. Scientific management, or 'Taylorism', is derived from six basic activities, as shown in Table 1.2.

Scientific management improved productivity in an era of mass production, but the emphasis was on quantity rather than on quality of production. Scientific management also identified work design, rewards, employee development and co-operation—all still important in modern organisations. Aspects of Taylorism are still visible in some manufacturing organisations today, for example a specialised machinist operating one machine at one particular work station. Scientific management applied to the built environment has given rise to the development of techniques for the control of construction time, cost, resources and project finance and ultimately treating the overall construction process as an integrated system. Thorough control is used from the inception stage to the completion of construction work.

One of the main disadvantages of scientific management was that it failed to take the human or social context of workers into account. Instead, Taylorist managers believed that pay was the most important reward for employees and, accordingly, assumed that the more workers earned the happier they would be. Scientific management also took the thinking out of work for the workers and treated them as another tool in the organisation, or as automatons. Scientific management theorists, however, did not sufficiently take into account the actual needs of workers in relation to matters such as working conditions, job satisfaction and having a say in matters which directly affected them.

Other contributors to scientific management who extended Taylor's work included, for example, Henry Gantt (1861–1919), and a husband and wife team, Frank Gilbreth (1868–1925) and Lillian Gilbreth (1878–1972). These theorists made significant contributions to the study of work.

Gantt's main contribution to management theory was the Gantt chart, in which a worker's progress was recorded. There are many variations of the Gantt chart; an example is given in Figure 1.2. The Gantt chart is one of the most frequently used methods of scheduling and control in the built environment. It lays out tasks associated with a given project and can be applied to most projects ranging from a company's marketing strategy to planning a major building project.

The chart was originally set up to indicate graphically the extent to which a worker had or had not achieved his or her assigned tasks. The chart was divided horizontally into hours, days, or weeks, with the task indicated by a straight line across the appropriate time span. The amount of the task achieved was shown by another straight line parallel to the original.

Figure 1.2 Gantt chart

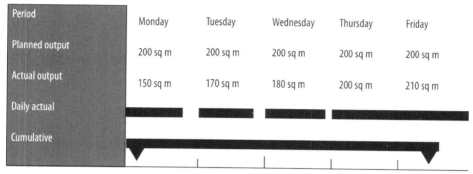

Period	Monday	Tuesday	Wednesday	Thursday	Friday
Planned output	200 sq m	200 sq m	200 sq m	200 sq m	200 sq m
Actual output	150 sq m	170 sq m	180 sq m	200 sq m	210 sq m
Daily actual					
Cumulative					

Gantt also introduced a payment system where performance below what was planned on the worker's chart still qualified the worker for the day rate, but achievement of the actual planned work earned the worker a large bonus. From this payment system, Gantt discovered that if one worker realised that the task could be achieved, many other workers quickly accomplished similar achievements, which resulted in workers learning for themselves and making greater use of their time. Gantt also believed that there was not just 'one best way' of completing a task, but a way 'which seems to be the best at the moment'.

The husband and wife team of Frank and Lillian Gilbreth used scientific management principles to eliminate unnecessary movements for bricklayers. The Gilbreths observed, for example, that as a direct result of analysing and redesigning the work methods of some bricklayers, the number of movements in laying bricks was reduced from eighteen to five per brick. The Gilbreths' focus was less on time than on the elimination of unnecessary movements, which became known as 'motion study'.

Henri Fayol

Henri Fayol (1841–1925) was a French mining engineer who believed that his fourteen principles of management were applicable to any organisation and were capable of adaptation according to need. He observed that these principles were the ones that he had to apply most frequently during his career. Table 1.3 shows the principles listed in the order set out by Fayol.

Table 1.3 Fayol's fourteen principles of management

Principle	Description
1. Division of Work	Increases productivity using the same effort.
2. Authority	The right to give orders and have orders followed.
3. Discipline	Fair agreements between employers and employees.
4. Unity of Command	Clear recognition of one person giving orders to reduce tension.
5. Unity of Direction	One person planning for group activities with a shared objective.
6. Subordination of Individual to Group Interest	Ensures employees achieve organisational goals rather than their own.
7. Remuneration	Pay should be fair to employees and organisations.
8. Centralisation	Incorporating both centralisation and decentralisation in order to achieve organisational goals efficiently.
9. Scalar Chain	The line of authority from top to bottom of organisations.
10. Order	The right people in the right place for the right job.
11. Equity	Fair treatment of all employees.
12. Stability of Tenure	Reducing inefficiency by having stable tenure (for example, permanent jobs or long-term contracts).
13. Initiative	All employees encouraged to show initiative.
14. Esprit de Corps (Team Spirit)	Contacts within and between departments should be encouraged. (Many companies in the built environment claim to use this philosophy, but in order to create unity and harmony, a deep understanding of and co-operation at all levels of management is needed.)

Fayol's principles have been criticised for being incapable of meeting the demands of dynamic modern organisations, but it is important to recognise that they were written in a different era. Fayol's principles of management, for example, take a perspective that looks at organisations from the top downwards, emphasising their hierarchical aspects. Fayol was the first theorist to devise a set of management principles which could be passed on to others. Fayol's principles, therefore, had more widespread applications for organisations than Taylor's scientific management, which was largely centred on the shop floor.

In Fayol's era, professionals in the built environment managed their organisations based on their experience and did not apply his principles. Later, however, this practice changed as management was recognised as a profession and theorists such as Fayol were studied for their contribution to management practice.

In Ireland, in the early 1900s contractors worked as 'trade contractors', directly employing skilled craftsmen and labourers; the management philosophy was autocratic and focused mainly on work output. In the mid-1900s, however, construction projects became larger and more technologically advanced as the era of material science and system building impacted on the construction industry, first in Britain and subsequently in Ireland. Clients required greater commercial performance from design teams and contractors in terms of time, cost and quality. Consequently, management systems were needed to deliver building projects under these new standards. The built environment industry changed its approach to management by developing construction project management as an integral element of the management of projects; site managers became accepted as management specialists; and management theories such as Fayol's principles of management were adopted.

Max Weber and the ideal–typical bureaucracy

Max Weber (1984–1920) was a German sociologist, rather than a practising manager like Taylor and Fayol. Weber took up the scientific management idea that there is 'one best way' to do a job and argued that there must be 'one best way' to run an organisation. He was particularly interested in managing the total organisation and in examining the structure of organisations and investigating why employees obey those in authority. Weber was not the first theorist to use the term **bureaucracy**, but in his writings he detailed the attributes of bureaucracy that still exist today (Table 1.4). Weber suggested the need for impersonal and rational management in charge of a bureaucratic organisation.

Table 1.4 Weber's elements of bureaucracy

Principle	Description
Division of Labour	Clear definitions of authority and responsibility as official duties.
Organisation of Positions into a Hierarchy	With each under the authority of a higher position.
People are Assigned to Positions in the Hierarchy	According to qualifications, assessment by examination or training and experience.
Decisions and Actions are Recorded in Writing	With files providing continuity and memory over time.
Management and Ownership	Are separated.
All are Subject to Rules and Procedures	Applied impersonally and equally to all to ensure predictability.

Weber believed that bureaucracy was necessary for the needs of large-scale organisations, enabling organisations to be both more efficient and adaptable to change. He believed in the *rational–legal model* of an organisation: **rational** because managers made decisions according to clear criteria; and **legal** because those in authority were appointed by a legitimate process. Bureaucracy, however, has become associated with 'red tape'—excessive rules and paperwork leading to inefficiency. It is important to remember that Weber's emphasis was on improving efficiency and this was suitable for organisations at that time, whereas modern organisations are more concerned with issues such as innovation and flexibility. Companies in the built environment tend to be less bureaucratic than those in manufacturing industries. The construction process has to allow for a large number of variables; so excessive bureaucracy can prove uneconomical.

Assessment of the classical management perspective

The classical perspective deserves credit for focusing serious attention on the importance of effective management. Many of the concepts developed during this era, such as job specialisation, time and motion studies, and scientific methods, are still used today. On the other hand, these early theorists often took a simplistic view of management and failed to understand the human element of organisations.

CONTRIBUTIONS

- Laid the foundation for later developments in management theory.
- Identified important management processes, functions, and skills that are still recognised as such today.
- Focused attention on management as a valid subject of scientific inquiry.

LIMITATIONS

- More appropriate for stable and simple organisations than for today's dynamic and complex organisations.
- Often prescribed universal procedures that are not appropriate in some settings.
- Employees were generally viewed as tools rather than as resources.

The human relations perspective

As outlined above, the classical management perspective emphasised organisational structures, and many classical management theorists viewed employees as part of the mechanics of organisations. In contrast, the human relations and social psychological theorists emphasised the importance of the human factor at work. In particular, individual attitudes and behaviours of groups were regarded as important. Human relations theorists were concerned with the motivation of employees, suggesting that employees are motivated by factors other than pay. (Motivation is discussed in Chapter 7.)

The **Hawthorne studies**, some of the most significant studies supporting the behavioural management perspective, were carried out by **Elton Mayo** and his associates between 1927 and 1932 at the Hawthorne plant of the Western Electric

Company in Chicago. The emphasis in the Hawthorne studies was on the worker rather than on the work. The studies involved manipulating lighting for one group of workers (experimental group) and comparing productivity in that group with another group's productivity where the lighting was not changed. Interestingly, productivity continued to increase in both groups, even when the lighting for the experimental group was decreased.

The main conclusions to be drawn from the Hawthorne studies are as follows.

- The need to belong to a group in the workplace is much more important than previous theorists had realised.
- Individual workers cannot be treated in isolation and must be seen as members of a group.
- Managers and employers need to be aware of the social needs of employees in organisations and to cater for those needs.
- Belonging to a group and having recognition within that group is as important as monetary incentives or good physical working conditions.

The emphasis on employees' social or belonging needs, in contrast to the tasks to be fulfilled, began during this era and is still considered to be very important in organisations today.

The Hawthorne experiment began as a study into physical working conditions, but developed as a series of studies into social factors, such as membership of groups and relationships with supervisors. As a result of the Hawthorne studies, the emphasis in organisations during the 1930s and 1940s changed from being task- or work-oriented to highlighting the social or belonging needs of employees. These concepts are still emphasised in management theories today. Further expansion of these human relations theories during the 1950s and 1960s by early motivational theorists such as Maslow, McGregor, Herzberg, and McClelland suggested that employees have far more than just physical and social needs to be satisfied. These theories are dealt with in detail in Chapter 7.

Companies in the built environment are now more aware of the needs and ambitions of employees and take a more human relations approach to the recruitment, welfare and development of staff. In 2008 and 2009, Davis Langdon PKS, a leading firm of construction consultants, was voted one of the top 50 Best Workplaces in Ireland in a poll run by Institute Ireland and the *Irish Independent*. Davis Langdon PKS (www.dlpks.ie) states:

In Davis Langdon PKS we focus on our values of integrity, innovation and collaboration and we are proud that all of our staff emulate these values.

Assessment of the human relations perspective

The human relations perspective focuses on employee behaviour in an organisational context. The human relations movement supplanted scientific management as the dominant approach to management in the 1930s and 1940s.

CONTRIBUTIONS
- Provided important insights into motivation, group dynamics and other interpersonal processes in organisations.
- Focused managerial attention on these processes.
- Challenged the view that employees are tools and furthered the belief that employees are valuable resources.

LIMITATIONS
- The complexity of individual behaviour makes prediction of that behaviour difficult.
- Many behavioural concepts have not yet been put to use because some managers are reluctant to adopt them.

The quantitative management perspective

Another management perspective, which emerged during the Second World War, was known as the quantitative management perspective. During this period, scientists and mathematicians solved military problems by using resources more efficiently and effectively. The achievements of this approach were also applied to organisations. Quantitative management concentrates on using mathematical and statistical models, and more recently computers, to achieve organisational efficiency and effectiveness. Kingspan, a leading international group of construction materials manufacturers, is a major user of high-end platform technologies in the design, manufacture, logistics and construction of building elements right through to complete buildings. Kingspan utilises much of mainstream manufacturing best practice and quantitative methodologies in its group of construction materials companies.

Quantitative management may be further subdivided into *management science* and *operations management*.

Management science involves the development of mathematical models and manipulating data to produce results. Management science also helps to solve organisational problems by using mixed teams of specialists who analyse problems and suggest various options by using complex statistical data in order to obtain greater understanding of problems. Management science encourages decision-making, based on the use of models, to obtain greater effectiveness. This is facilitated by the use of special computer packages.

Operations management is a transformation process that can be considered as a form of applied management science and is used (Naylor 2004):

to plan, organise, operate and control a transformation system that takes inputs from a variety of sources and produces outputs of goods and services at times and places defined by internal or external customers.

Operations management is concerned with making entire organisations more effective and efficient from the strategic management level down to the operating level. Operations management techniques can be applied to a wide range of activities, including forecasting, inventory management, and managing queues. Overall, quantitative management has provided managers with a number of decision-making tools and techniques which are particularly useful for planning and controlling and has increased understanding of overall organisational processes. It is important, however, to remember that mathematical models cannot predict or account for individual employee behaviour and attitude. Various mathematical models have been developed and are still in use by companies in the built environment. These include CPM (critical path method), PERT (project evaluation and review technique) and linear programming.

The **systems approach** is a management theory built around the idea of systems. A *system* is an interrelated set of elements functioning as a whole. The systems approach suggests that managers should focus on the role each part (or department) of an organisation plays in the whole organisation, rather than dealing separately with each part. The systems approach recognises the different needs of various departments: for example, the production manager may want to produce a variety of products, whereas the marketing manager may prefer to concentrate on one or two specialised products, and the finance manager may be primarily concerned with keeping costs to a minimum.

The systems approach stresses the importance of *subsystems*—systems within a broader system. The finance, production and marketing departments are not only systems in their own right but are also subsystems within an organisation. *Synergy* emphasises the interrelationships between all parts of an organisation, reflecting that organisational departments (or subsystems) may often be more successful working together than working alone. This suggests that departments and units in a business are more productive when they work together than when they operate separately.

The systems approach, therefore, means that managers have to discuss various requirements of each department in terms of meeting the needs of the whole organisation. This interaction requires a high degree of communication and the breaking down of barriers between the various departments and functions of an organisation. Griffin (2008) suggests that when organisations are viewed as systems, four basic elements can be identified:

- inputs
- transformation processes
- outputs
- feedback.

First, inputs are the resources an organisation gets from its environment, including raw materials, information, and financial and human resources. Site managers use these inputs by organising plant, materials and direct and sub-contracted labour on site to meet the short-term goals of a construction project, for example completing the substructure of a building before progressing to work on the superstructure.

Second, through managerial and technological processes the inputs are transformed into outputs. Outputs include flows of information, materials and human energy which move through a system and are transformed by various processes into products and services. General managers and contract managers set and balance the long-term project goals of a construction project with external pressures and constraints, which may come from the client or the government, in order to complete the project successfully.

Finally, feedback is the process of monitoring information about systems in order to evaluate their operation.

Applying the systems approach to the built environment involves distinguishing three different types of work to be undertaken by managers working for a construction contractor. Examples of these work types are detailed in Figure 1.3.

Figure 1.3 Systems theory applied to the built environment

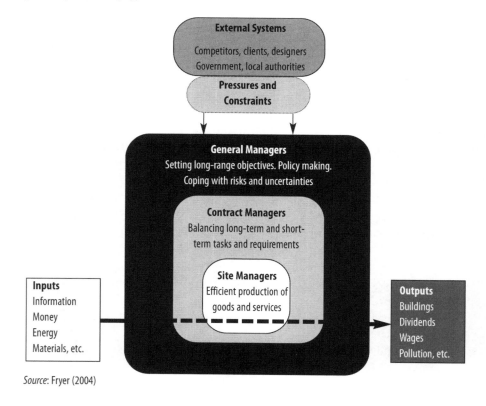

Source: Fryer (2004)

Assessment of the quantitative management perspective

The quantitative management perspective has provided managers with an abundance of decision-making tools and techniques and has increased understanding of overall organisational processes. It focuses on applying mathematical models and processes to management situations.

CONTRIBUTIONS

- Developed sophisticated quantitative techniques to assist in decision-making.
- Application of models has increased awareness and understanding of complex organisational processes and situations.
- Useful in the planning and controlling processes.

LIMITATIONS

- Cannot fully explain or predict the behaviour of people in organisations.
- Mathematical sophistication may come at the expense of other important skills.

The contingency management perspective

Theorists from the classical management perspective believed that there was 'one best way' to manage organisations and that once this 'best way' was found all could learn from it. In contrast, the contingency management perspective suggests that there is no 'one best way' to manage organisations, and aims to provide solutions to organisational management problems by responding to the unique circumstances involved. It recognises that in each situation there are common circumstances (those previously experienced by other organisations) *and* unique circumstances, and these may be looked at in combination to provide better solutions for particular problems. When a problem is examined, its solution will depend on its particular causes. The task for contingency management is to identify which solutions are most likely to work in given circumstances. The contingency management perspective has developed from attempts to apply various techniques to solve management problems, for example using the theories of the behavioural management perspective (with regard to motivation) together with quantitative analyses of findings.

Management in the built environment differs from other industries because of the nature of construction work. Each construction site is unique in terms of the variability of ground conditions, prevailing weather and the teams of people involved in the design and construction stages. Each construction site, therefore, requires a strong contingency management approach to deal with these variables. Figure 1.4 illustrates a contingency and risk management approach to a construction problem, namely contaminated soil on the site of a proposed project.

Risk management is a relatively new management approach to be adopted by construction clients and construction organisations in assisting in developing a contingency management capability. By analysing past projects to determine patterns of risk type and events such as soil conditions, material performances, building design and human resource performance, risk profiles, their probabilities and contingency plans can be developed. This greatly improves the management capability for construction organisations.

Figure 1.4 Construction sector risk diagram

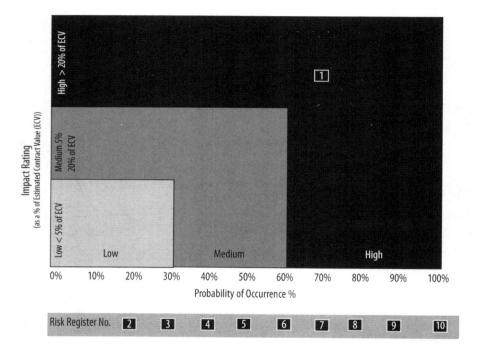

Figure 1.4 identifies the probability of contaminated soil on the site at 70%. Figure 1.4 illustrates the position of Risk 1 with a 70% probability of occurrence and a high impact rating of greater that 20% of the estimated contract value. This impact rating measures the financial impact the risk could have if it were to occur. A risk register is then prepared (see Figure 1.5), which gives details of:

- risk details
- risk description
- estimated cost if the risk occurs
- probability of occurrence
- estimated contingency value
- risk impact
- possible course of action
- selected course of action
- cost of risk treatment

- effect on contingency value
- risk management decision
- risk action status.

Figure 1.5 Construction sector risk register

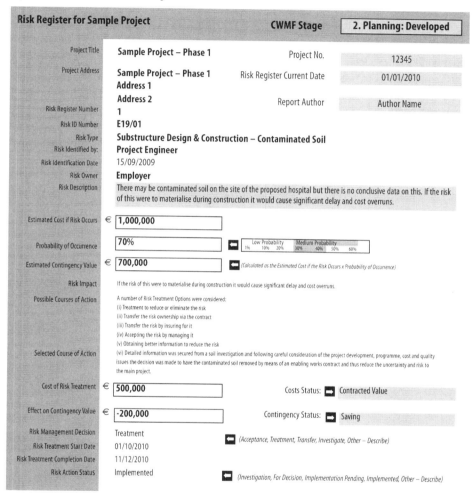

This type of risk management enables construction projects to be run in a more effective and planned manner.

Using the contingency management approach, managers consider the objectives of a particular action, the people involved, the equipment available, and internal and external conditions. Internal and external environments are dealt with in detail in Chapter 2. A number of theorists, such as Burns and Stalker, Lawrence and Lorsch, and Mintzberg, have studied links between organisational structures and other variables.

Burns and Stalker

From the late 1950s, British behavioural scientists Tom Burns and G. M. Stalker have examined how organisations adjust to changing environmental conditions. Burns and Stalker characterised organisations as being mechanistic organisations or organic organisations. **Mechanistic organisations** tend to have rigid structures and can be similar to bureaucracies. **Organic organisations**, in contrast, tend to be flexible in structure and adaptive to change (see Table 1.5 for a summary of the characteristics). Construction companies, like many other commercial organisations, exhibit elements of both organisational types. They tend to be mechanistic in terms of their planning and execution of work when predictions of weather, resource management and finance are not deviating from expectations. On the other hand, when these variables deviate significantly, many construction companies can adapt an organic response to changes in the work environment. Some construction companies, however, that operate a mechanistic-type organisation find it difficult to respond to a changing construction environment and consequently fail to adapt in time; and this invariably leads to company closure.

Table 1.5 Characteristics of mechanistic and organic organisations

Mechanistic	Organic
Tasks are specialised, precise and narrow.	Tasks are more independent and imprecise.
Tasks tend to be rigid, unless altered formally by top management.	Tasks are adjusted and redefined by employees.
Information relevant to particular situations and running the organisation lies with the chief executive.	Information is generated throughout the organisation.
Communication is usually between superior and subordinate (vertical) in relation to issuing orders and instructions.	Communication is both vertical and horizontal (between peers) and is used for information and advice.
Loyalty to the organisation and obedience to superiors is expected.	Loyalty is to project and teamwork.

Burns and Stalker suggested that they did not view one or other system as being superior, but that organisations could move from one system to the other as external organisational conditions changed. They believed that what was important was gaining the most appropriate system for the particular circumstances.

Lawrence and Lorsch

The work of Lawrence and Lorsch, first published in the United States in 1967, was influenced by Burns and Stalker. Their study began with an investigation of the degree of **differentiation** (dividing organisations into functions such as production, sales, finance, etc.) and **integration** (achieving collaboration between departments to achieve overall unity) in six organisations in the plastics industry and their rapidly changing environments.

Lawrence and Lorsch believed that both mechanistic *and* organic types of organisations were crucial for coping with environmental diversity, whereas Burns and Stalker believed that organic systems were more appropriate for changing conditions. Lawrence and Lorsch suggested that, in rapidly changing environmental situations, large organisations still have to maintain structure and formality. They also believed that most organisations are in a state of tension as a result of the need to be both differentiated and integrated.

This tension is evident among construction companies that have created mechanistic organisational structures and procedures for running their businesses. As the recession impacts on their workload there is a strong need for these companies to become more organic to enable them to adapt to the changing market, to develop new products and services for their clients and to compete with their competitors.

Supply and demand for construction activity is largely based on derived demand. Derived demand is a by-product of the general economy: if the economy is doing well there will be strong demand for private and public buildings, roads and housing. Conversely, in periods of recession, demand for construction tends to reduce relative to the prevailing market. The speed and severity of the recent recession has alarmed many economic observers. The subsequent drop in derived demand for construction activity has severely tested the ability of construction companies to adapt quickly to the changing market. Many smaller construction companies are experiencing difficulties in readjusting quickly enough and are becoming insolvent. Larger construction companies are downsizing their organisational structures to a minimum to enable their costs to be reduced and thus allow for competitive pricing of projects. This downsizing process, however, is difficult and is being done in a state of tension, or as Lawrence and Lorsch have described it, the need to be both differentiated and integrated.

Henry Mintzberg

Henry Mintzberg developed the concept of an organisation structure composed of various segments (summarised in Figure 1.6). Mintzberg contends that six basic components are found in organisations:

- the *strategic apex* running the whole organisation
- the *middle-line managers* connecting the operating core with the apex, such as commercial and contracts managers
- the *technostructure* designing and controlling processes, for example engineers, information specialists, accountants, consultants
- the *support staff* providing direct services, for example public relations, transport, canteen, cleaning, secretarial and technical staff

- the *operating core* producing goods or services such as the site manager and operatives on a building site
- the *ideology* binding the whole together.

According to Mintzberg, each organisation is dominated by a different component part. For example, the owner–manager entrepreneurial organisation is dominated by the strategic apex. In contrast, a skilled professional organisation, such as property auctioneers, works directly on outputs.

Figure 1.6 Mintzberg's model of an organisation structure

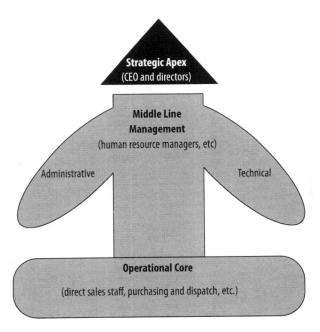

Peters and Waterman

Thomas Peters and Robert Waterman investigated sixty-two major American organisations that had performed excellently during the period 1961 to 1980. Their book, *In Search of Excellence: Lessons from America's Best-run Companies*, shows eight management excellence characteristics not generally exhibited by organisations that did not perform as well:

- a bias for action—moving on rather than being slowed by analysis
- closeness to the customer—learning from the people served
- autonomy and entrepreneurship—fostering innovators and risk takers
- productivity through people—participation as a basis for rising standards

- a hands-on, value-driven approach—all stakeholders know what the company stands for, leaders get involved at all levels
- sticking to the knitting—focus on business known to participants
- a simple form, lean staff—a minimum of headquarters staff to run a large business through simpler organisation structures
- simultaneous loose–tight properties—being as decentralised as possible while centralising the things that really matter.

Managers are now encouraged to recognise the ability of the people they manage and to devolve decision-making as far as possible. This suggests that the people who have to implement a decision should make it by analysing the situation and deciding on courses of action. This should result in the contingency approach being carried to successful conclusions.

It is clear that the contingency management approach needs to analyse each situation and then draw on various schools of management theory in order to decide on the most appropriate combination. The contingency approach helps managers to be aware of the complexity in any situation and to take an active role in trying to determine what would work best in each situation, against the background of rapidly changing external environments.

1.4 Key points

Management is a set of functions directed at achieving organisational goals efficiently and effectively. These basic functions include:

- planning
- decision-making
- organising
- leading
- controlling.

Modern-day management theories have emerged from a combination of approaches to management which have been developed over the last hundred years.

The *classical management* perspective consisted of scientific management and administrative management. Overall, the classical management perspective was concerned with improving organisational efficiency and work methods for individual workers but had little regard for employees.

The *human relations* perspective was concerned with individual and group behaviour. This perspective emerged primarily as a result of the Hawthorne studies. The approach recognised the importance of group behaviour for employees in organisations and highlighted the fact that employees are also motivated by non-monetary factors.

The *quantitative management* perspective consists of management science and operations management. This perspective applies quantitative techniques in attempting to solve problems and make decisions.

The *contingency management* perspective suggests that there is no universal approach to managing organisations, as organisational management depends on (or is contingent upon) each individual situation. Contingency management theorists are concerned with the links between organisational structures and other variables together with many other modern-day management issues.

Table 1.6 Summary of management theories

Classical management, late 1890s to 1914	
Taylor	Scientific management
Gantt	The Gantt chart
Gilbreth and Gilbreth	Motion study
Fayol	Management principles
Weber	Bureaucracy
Behavioural management, 1900 to 1940	
Mayo	Hawthorne studies
McGregor	Theory X, Theory Y (see Chapter 7)
Maslow	Hierarchy of needs (see Chapter 7)
Quantitative management 1940+	Management science
	Operations management
Contingency management 1980+	Organisational behaviour
Burns and Stalker	Mechanistic and organic organisations
Lawrence and Lorsch	Differentiation and integration of organisations
Mintzberg	Organisational structure
Peters and Waterman	Characteristics of excellent organisations

Important terms and concepts

bureaucracy (p. 9)
classical management perspective (p. 4)
commanding (p. 2)
construction project management (p. 9)
contingency management perspective (p. 15)
controlling (p. 2)
co-ordinating (p. 2)
effective (p. 2)

efficient (p. 2)
Fayol's principles of management (p. 1)
first-line managers (p. 4)
forecasting (p. 1)
Gantt chart (p. 7)
Hawthorne studies (p. 10)
human relations perspective (p. 11)
management defined (p. 1)
management science (p. 12)
mechanistic organisation (p. 18)
middle managers (p. 3)
Mintzberg's organisational types (p. 19)
operations management (p. 12)
organic organisation (p. 18)
organising (p. 1)
planning (p. 1)
quantitative management perspective (p. 21)
risk management (p. 15)
risk register (p. 17)
systems approach (p. 13)
Taylor's principles of scientific management (p. 5)
top managers (p. 3)
trade contractors (p. 9)
Weber's elements of bureaucracy (p. 9)

Questions for review

1. Critically compare and contrast the contributions made by the classical management perspective and the behavioural management perspective. Include the primary contributors to each of these theories.
2. Illustrate the importance of forecasting, planning, organising, co-ordinating and controlling for an organisation working in the built environment.
3. Discuss the relevance of Fayol's principles of management for modern organisations in the built environment.
4. Write brief notes on the following:
   a. the Hawthorne studies
   b. bureaucracy
   c. quantitative management perspective
   d. contingency management perspective.
5. Outline the benefits to an organisation in the built environment of adopting a human relations approach to managing its workforce.

6. Describe how systems theory could be applied to a construction company for the purpose of a new building project for a client.
7. In a rapidly changing recessionary period, evaluate how mechanistic and organic characteristics can affect a construction company attempting to adapt to this environment.
8. Illustrate how Mintzberg's model of an organisation structure could be applied to a large-scale construction company in Ireland.

2
THE ORGANISATIONAL ENVIRONMENT

Learning outcomes

Following study of this chapter you will be able to:
- describe the main forces of the external environment and show how they impact on built environment organisations
- describe the main forces of the internal (or task) environment and show how they impact on built environment organisations
- explain how Porter's 'five forces' determine industry profitability
- understand Porter's 'three generic strategies'.

2.1 The organisational environment defined

All societies are influenced by managers and their organisations. Managers need to have a clear understanding of the environment in which their organisations function (see Table 2.1).

Table 2.1 Organisations in society and the built environment

Organisations in Society	Organisations in the Built Environment
Hospitals	Sanctioning authorities and sponsoring agencies (employers)
Schools	Planning and regulatory authorities
Government agencies	Environmental agencies and groups
Business organisations	Built environment professional firms
Voluntary groups	Construction companies and materials suppliers
Religious groups	Financial and property asset companies

An organisation has been defined (Griffin 2008) as:

> a group of people working together in a structured and co-ordinated fashion to achieve a set of goals.

All organisations interact with the environment in which they operate. Everything that customers, companies and other institutions do will have some impact on the environment. The environment is composed of a number of elements that can determine the success or failure of an organisation. The environment of an organisation may be defined as: *all those elements that lie outside and inside the organisation's boundary with which the organisation interacts.* From this definition it is apparent that an organisation operates in both an **external** (*macro*) and **internal** (*task/project*) environment. An organisation can also operate in an **international** environment (global).

2.2 The external environment

The external environment consists of elements that lie outside an organisation and have the potential to influence that organisation in significant ways (see Figure 2.1). Organisations cannot determine external environmental factors, such as a nation's recession or boom period. The external environment comprises elements that can be divided into four main groupings, known by the acronym **STEP**:

- the **social** environment
- the **technological** environment
- the **economic** environment
- the **political–legal** environment.

Figure 2.1 Forces in the external and internal environments—STEP

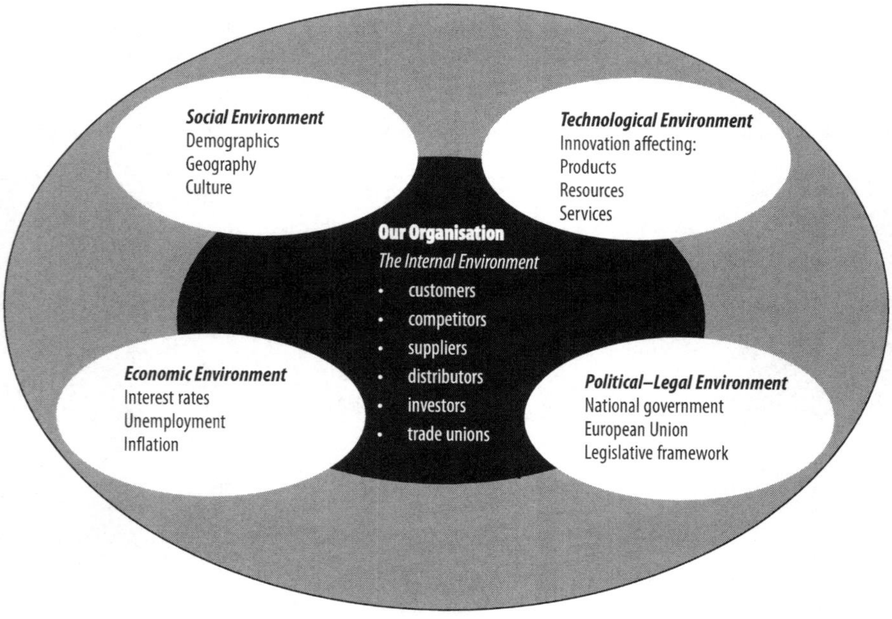

Social Environment
Demographics
Geography
Culture

Technological Environment
Innovation affecting:
Products
Resources
Services

Our Organisation
The Internal Environment
- customers
- competitors
- suppliers
- distributors
- investors
- trade unions

Economic Environment
Interest rates
Unemployment
Inflation

Political–Legal Environment
National government
European Union
Legislative framework

The social environment

The social, societal or socio-cultural environment refers to the elements that generally make up society. These elements include the *demographic, geographic* and *cultural factors* in which an organisation operates. Social processes influence organisations in servicing demands for products and services, and also influence standards of organisational conduct according to the respective societal values in which differing organisations operate. Religion, for example, can be an important cultural determinant and influence on a society. The social environment can impact on the built environment, in both the public and private sectors. Society can determine a demand for building and for different types of facilities such as housing, schools and roads.

The social environment, however, can go through significant changes, even during a decade. According to Turley (1986), the importance of Irish religious institutions in determining culture was found to be above the European average in the 1980s, whereas a survey conducted in 1998 showed a marked decline in the centrality of religion to Irish society (RTÉ 1998). Other significant social changes in Ireland during the 1990s included the introduction of divorce and the decriminalisation of homosexual practices; and in the current decade, there is growing societal and legal support for full civil partnerships for heterosexual and gay couples.

Society is also influenced by international trends, and the development of environmental awareness has followed these trends in recent years. The social environment in Ireland is adapting to the need for more sustainable practices in the way people live in the natural environment.

The social environment determines the goods, services and standards that society values. Social changes have an impact on the built environment, for example in the housing sector the increase in one-parent families has an impact on the need for social housing. Society can also determine other changes in client requirements, for example the multi-storey housing used as a solution to housing shortages during the 1970s. This trend is now reversed in recent years with the supply of more mixed housing units and apartment blocks. Additionally, the increased awareness of environmental issues such as energy use, CO_2 emissions, climate change, and flooding has resulted in better standards for the planning, design and construction of buildings and infrastructures.

Demographic factors

Demographic factors include:
- population
- age structure
- income distribution.

Population changes affect the demand for products and services; for example, since the average expected life span is now greater than in previous generations, the supply of health care services and facilities for the elderly has greatly increased. The shift in the Irish population from rural areas to cities also affects infrastructural services, such as transport systems, housing and schools. These services and facilities need to be of high quality to meet the safety requirements of the end user. Where a housing development is being undertaken, planners need to ensure that sufficient facilities such as schools and crèches will be available to the new house owners. *Age structure* also has an influence on an organisation's environment; for example, during a baby boom period the demand for child-related products and services increases. *Income distribution* also influences the environmental factors of an organisation; for example, the demand for luxury items and non-essential services are directly affected when the members of the society in which an organisation operates experience changes to their disposable income.

Home buyers will have different perceptions about what they expect from a new home, often dependent on their disposable income and size of family. Show houses will need to be presented differently to various target segments of potential buyers. Families with children will expect bedrooms to be big enough for children's toys; and the choice and design of fitted furniture will be influenced by the tastes and disposable income of the potential buyer.

Geographic factors

These include:
- transport infrastructure
- climate
- sources of energy
- language

and have an influence on the operations of an organisation. In Ireland, for instance, many organisations are based close to the seaports and airports of Dublin, Cork and Shannon, and many American organisations prefer to set up operations in the European Union in the English-speaking environments of Ireland or Britain. The National Spatial Plan (2002), which is a twenty-year national planning framework for Ireland, aims to deliver more sustainable regional development during the period covered by the plan. The plan aims to improve people's quality of life and deliver better areas to live in.

Cultural factors

Cultural factors, such as:
- values
- social norms
- the prevailing attitudes of a population

influence the environment in which an organisation operates. Differences in culture arise from nationality, gender, social class, education, religious background and age. National culture in all countries remains very strong and successful managers have to be prepared to adapt to local environments. Attitudes and social values that determine a culture are constantly changing in all countries, and managers also have to be adaptable to these changing factors. Organisations took time to adapt to the cultural diversity created by the influx of foreign workers into the construction sector during the boom years of the late 1990s and early 2000s. While the construction industry in Ireland has gone into steep decline since 2007, it still remains culturally diverse and this diversity is now valued as an asset when Irish construction firms tender for work abroad.

Cultural changes in relation to customer demands in the built environment are also evident. One of the most noticeable developments in this area is that clients and end users are now more environmentally aware. Renewable technologies are now popular, and the construction industry has been adapting to these changes, for example by developing the building energy rating system.

The technological environment

According to Griffin (2008), 'technological environment' refers to the methods available for converting resources into products or services. Technology affects the operation of internal organisational environments, and relies on technology which is available in external environments. Technological environments are rapidly changing, with noticeable advances in organisations, ranging from information communication technologies (ICT) to bio-engineering technology in human health sciences and foods, from Internet technologies developing business and networking opportunities to computer modelling technologies for large-scale building design, and nanotechnology systems and structures for industry and science.

The built environment now has a large range of technologies and design tools to enable greater modelling and testing of projects prior to construction. Common standards and practices in the commissioning of projects, however, are not uniform in Ireland and this needs to be developed if the full benefits of design, manufacture and facilities management technologies are to be utilised and co-ordinated. There is an urgent need for standards in computer-aided design drawings to have prescribed layering conventions so that the various design disciplines can co-ordinate their designs and avoid unnecessary conflicts at construction/manufacturing stages.

The economic environment

The economic dimension of the external environment refers to the overall conditions in which an organisation operates. The economic environment influences the costs of operating in different locations, for example the cost of labour in a particular country. Other factors that influence the economic environment include:

- inflation
- interest rates
- unemployment
- per capita income.

The current economic recession in Ireland has seen a reversal of the Celtic Tiger period of the late 1990s to 2007, resulting in high unemployment, falling gross national product, growing government shortfalls for day-to-day expenditure and an unprecedented financial crisis in banking institutions (see Chapter 10). As creators of fixed capital in the form of buildings and roads, the construction and civil engineering sectors have experienced particular difficulties with rapid decline in employment, output and revenues. These sectors must now adopt lean management practices to reduce costs, and undergo major organisational restructuring to enable companies in the sectors to fit the current market and to enable future growth. The CRH case study on page 175 illustrates how an Irish company can adapt to the changing economic environment.

The political–legal environment

The political–legal environment refers to government regulations imposed on organisations and the legal framework established for operations. In Ireland, organisations operate under Irish and European Union laws. EU member states have to adhere to common decisions on, for example, fishing, agriculture, trade, economics and the physical environment.

The built environment is a heavily regulated sector in terms of the legislative frameworks applied to designs, planning approval, building regulations, health and safety, sustainability, energy and carbon profiles, and statutory licensing and consents. Table 2.2 presents an example of the consents and licence requirements for public work contracts.

Table 2.2 Consents and licence requirements for public works contracts

Item	Consent/Licence
1	Outline Planning Permission
2	Planning Permission under the Planning and Development Act 2000
3	Part 8 Planning and Development Regulations 2001
4	Part 9 Planning and Development Regulations 2001
5	Compulsory Purchase Orders (i.e. in accordance with the Housing Act 1966)
6	Toll Scheme (Section 57 of the Roads Acts 1993 as amended)
7	Motorways Scheme Orders under the Roads Act 1993 (as amended)
8	Wayleaves (Section 43 Gas Act 1976)
9	Foreshore Licence under the Foreshore Acts 1933–2003
10	Dumping at Sea Permit – Dumping at Sea Act 2004 (No. 35)
11	Agreements with state or semi-state bodies (i.e. ESB, Coillte, NRA, OPW, Irish Rail)

12	Rights of way/consents in relation to habitats, Special Areas of Conservation (SACs), Natural Heritage Areas (NHAs) (Wildlife Acts 1976–2000, Council Directives 79/409 EEC, 82/72 EEC, 92/43 EEC)
13	Tree felling licence (Forestry Act 1946)
14	Approval of local fisheries boards (Fisheries, Tidal Waters Act 1934)
15	Appropriate licences/consents under the National Monuments Acts 1930–2004
16	Bridge Order required in certain circumstances from Minister for the Environment, Heritage and Local Government (Local Government Act 1946)
17	Consent of the Commissioners of Public Works to all new bridge proposals under Section 50 Arterial Drainage (Amendment) Act 1995
18	Railway Order (Transport Railway Infrastructure Act 2001)
19	Canal By-laws (Canal Act 1986 (By-laws) 1988)
20	Position of vehicle/mobile crane/hoist application
21	Temporary Road Closure Application (Section 75 of the Roads Act 1993)
22	Road opening licence/T-2 Licence (S13 subsection 109b of the Roads Act 1993)
23	Hoarding/Scaffolding Licence
24	Abnormal Indivisible Load (Road Traffic (Construction and Use of Vehicle) Regulations 2003)
25	Effluent discharge licence

Source: *Capital Works Management Framework Guidance Note 1.5 (Ver. 1.1) Public Works Contracts*, Department of Finance, 2009.

2.3 The internal environment

The internal environment is also referred to as the *operating environment* or the *task environment*. Factors that are part of the internal environment and that affect organisational behaviour include:

- customers
- competitors
- suppliers
- distributors
- investors
- trade unions
- professional bodies (e.g. Engineers Ireland, Society of Chartered Surveyors, Royal Institute of Architects of Ireland and Chartered Institute of Builders)
- industry representative organisations (e.g. the Construction Industry Federation).

Customers

Managers have to decide the answers to two fundamental questions:

1. *What business are we in?*

2. *Who are our customers?*

And when an organisation begins to ask itself: '*What "line of business" are we actually in?*' it is beginning to identify its potential customers.

By asking these questions it is clear that an organisation is identifying **marketing** as an important management function. Once the organisation understands the business it is in, doing what it is good at ('sticking to the knitting') becomes clear. The organisation can then begin to segment and target the various markets and then position its product(s) for those customers it wishes to serve. An organisation's customers can include:

- individuals—who may be buying products/services for their own consumption
- other companies—who may be interested in buying products/services
- government departments.

It is important for an organisation to know its customers in order to meet their requirements by having *the right product, at the right place, at the right time.* The many clients of the built environment have a variety of reasons for constructing new buildings: for example, a private sector client who wishes to sell or rent property in anticipation of a financial return; a manufacturer who builds a new factory and is expecting a productivity gain; and a public sector client who would expect a return on a social investment from a new school.

Construction markets are classified by the Department of the Environment, Heritage and Local Government as:

1. Residential construction
   - Private housing
   - Public housing
2. Non-residential construction
   - Industry
   - Commercial
   - Agricultural
   - Tourism
   - Worship
3. Productive infrastructure
   - Roads
   - Water services
   - Airports/seaports
   - Energy
   - Transport
   - Communications
4. Social infrastructure
   - Education

- Health
- Public buildings.

Competitors

The competitors of an organisation are other organisations that compete with it for revenue. As organisations operating in the same industry compete for the same customers, managers must anticipate and react to the strategies of competitors in order to remain competitive. Competition in the construction sector, for example, has increased dramatically with the decline in work volumes; fewer contracts are available, so companies must develop business models, tendering strategies and organisational structures that enable them to compete for market share.

Suppliers

Suppliers are organisations that provide resources for other organisations. Supplies vary and can include:
- capital goods
- vehicles
- equipment
- raw materials
- finance
- personnel, provided through agencies or by sub-contract.

Most organisations use several suppliers simultaneously because having a sole supplier brings a higher risk if that company goes out of business. Losing a key supplier of raw materials can mean that production flow is interrupted or a lower-quality product or more expensive substitution has to be made. Choosing suppliers, negotiating terms and building professional working relationships are tasks that managers have to perform frequently. Work in the built environment is heavily dependent on suppliers such as Tobermore for paving products and Cemex for concrete. Suppliers can be domestic or nominated with pre-approved procedures in place for ordering and delivery of materials.

Distributors

Distribution involves handling and moving out-bound goods from an organisation to customers. Distribution may be direct, using company-owned transport, or indirect, using external agents or brokers. The distributors' task is to ensure that the right product will be at the right place at the right time, and the choice of distribution channel is determined by the needs of customers as well as by knowledge of particular markets. The choice of distributors also has to be consistent with the needs and capabilities of an organisation. Concrete, for example, is a product that requires an efficient and effective distribution system. The distribution of concrete is generally organised by a concrete manufacturing facility which batches the concrete to the prescribed mix required by the customer. The delivery vehicles are normally privately owned by independent operators who deliver and pour the concrete where the client requires it.

Investors

Investors include banks and other financial institutions, which provide short-term finance to shareholders, or lenders of long-term capital who have a long-term commitment.

Trade unions

According to Gunnigle *et al.* (1999), trade unions are seen as an effective means of achieving satisfactory pay and working conditions for employees. Trade unions aim to ensure that employees are treated fairly by employers. The basic strength of a trade union lies in its ability to organise and unite workers. The main objectives of trade unions are to:
- achieve satisfactory levels of pay and conditions of employment
- provide members with a range of services
- strengthen employee bargaining power by replacing individual bargaining with collective bargaining
- reflect the interests of wage earners or workers.

Workers in the built environment are generally represented by craft, industrial or general trade unions.

Craft unions: membership is based on a particular skill gained after a period of training or apprenticeship. Members are represented by BATU (Building and Allied Trades' Union).

Industrial: membership is based on a particular industry. Members are represented by TEEU (Technical Engineering and Electrical Union).

General: membership is broadly based, normally across several industries. Members are represented by SIPTU (Services, Industrial, Professional and Technical Union). See Chapter 8 for more on trade unions.

Professional bodies and construction employer organisations in the built environment

A professional body is an organisation in a particular profession which aims to establish and maintain professional standards in order to protect the interests of its members and the interests of the public. Table 2.3 provides examples of various professional bodies in the built environment. Customers hiring members of a professional body can be confident that they are employing people who have a professional qualification and who are undertaking lifelong learning through career development.

Table 2.3 Professional bodies in the built environment

Professional Body	Represented Parties
Chartered Institute of Building (CIOB) (www.ciob.org.uk)	Represents various professionals in the built environment. The CIOB has over 2,800 members in the Irish branch. The body aims to: • serve its members effectively • raise the institute's profile in Ireland.
Engineers Ireland (www.iei.ie)	Represents over 24,000 engineers from all disciplines in Ireland. Aims to: • promote knowledge of engineering • establish and maintain standards of professional engineering and engineering education • provide opportunities for continuing professional development (CPD) for engineers • maintain standards of professional ethics and conduct • ensure that professional titles are granted to qualified candidates • act as the authoritative voice of the engineering profession in Ireland.
Irish Auctioneers and Valuers Institute (IAVI) (www.iavi.ie).	Represents over 1,400 qualified property professionals. Aims to 'promote the highest professional, ethical and educational standards in the property industry'.
Royal Institute of the Architects of Ireland (RIAI) (www.riai.ie)	Represents qualified architects in Ireland. Promotes the highest standards in architecture and provides impartial and authoritative advice and information on issues affecting architects, the built environment and society. Aims to maintain high standards of professional practice by: • setting standards of knowledge, skill and competence for practice • monitoring standards of admission to the profession • accrediting architectural and architectural technology courses • carrying out examinations in professional practice and in architectural technology • supporting continuing professional development for architects and architectural technologists • monitoring requirements for architectural education and training.

Society of Chartered Surveyors (SCS) (www.scs.ie)	Represents chartered surveyors operating in Ireland: over 1,800 qualified practising members. The SCS aims to: • promote the diverse knowledge of the profession • maintain the highest educational and professional standards • protect consumers through strict codes of practice • provide expert advice on property and built environment issues • be the state registration body for the titles of quantity surveyor and building surveyor under the Building Control Act 2007.

The construction employer organisation in Ireland is the Construction Industry Federation (CIF). The Construction Employers Federation (CEF) represents construction companies in Northern Ireland. Table 2.4 gives a brief summary of the services offered by each organisation.

Table 2.4 The Construction Industry Federation and the Construction Employers Federation

Construction Industry Federation (CIF) (www.cif.ie)	Professional body representing over 3,000 members in all areas of the built environment in Ireland. It represents companies of all sizes, from all sectors of the industry. The sectors are categorised into four main areas : • general contractors • mechanical and electrical contractors • specialist contractors • home builders. It offers a comprehensive range of services for members, including training and development in: • health and safety • management • tendering and contracting • energy and environmental issues • industrial relations, employment and manpower services.

Construction Employers Federation (CEF) (www.cefni.co.uk)	Represents over 1,300 companies of all sizes and across all sectors of the construction industry in Northern Ireland, from civil engineering to general construction, house building and repair and maintenance. Provides a wide range of services for all member companies, including:

- member liaisons: deals with important issues in all sectors of the industry through various committees and liaison groups

- courses and seminars aimed at both managers and construction professionals

- planning advice: free advice to full and associate members on planning issues

- free legal hotline: free legal advice for up to a half an hour on a wide range of legal topics

- health and safety support and advice: includes services such as site safety inspection, accident investigation management, courses and seminars, leaders in construction safety and best practice guidance

- environmental support and advice: professional advice to members on both general and legal environmental queries

- tax helpline: offers advice on business and taxation issues

- employment support: provides members with a range of information and assistance on employment issues such as wages, holidays, terms and conditions of employment

- tender query support: takes a proactive role in promoting and persuading clients to follow best practice tendering for construction projects.

2.4 The international environment

The international environment of an organisation is concerned with operating across national boundaries. Within the international environment there are multiple economic, social, cultural, legal, political, and technological environments. Managers have to make decisions regarding, for example, currency, shipping costs, import duties, and other taxes. Operating in the international environment, therefore, is far more complex than operating domestically.

Organisations that operate internationally need to pay special attention to varying socio-cultural factors, social structures, and customs. Many Irish companies operating in the built environment began to work internationally in countries such as Britain, France and Dubai during the boom years of the late 1990s and early 2000s. This led to problems with different cultures and practices relating to contractual arrangements, in particular, where contracts had been written in a different language and contained unfamiliar clauses.

Griffin (2008) views the international environment as the extent to which an organisation is involved in or is affected by business in other countries. Organisations that operate in only one country can also be affected by the international environment as they may face competition from foreign imports or may find it necessary to import raw materials to manufacture their product(s). For many Irish organisations the international environment is of increasing importance for both exporting and importing products. CRH (Cement Roadstone Holdings), for example, is Ireland's leading building materials company, which employs in excess of 90,000 people in thirty-five countries with group worldwide sales of €10 billion (www.crh.ie).

The transfer of employees from their home countries to host countries to work for a number of years is another aspect that many human resource managers have to deal with. The preparation, recruitment, selection and training of both staff members and their family members are some of the issues that have to be dealt with when employees move internationally.

In the European context, co-operation in trade and economic policies has an influence on Irish management policies. Ireland's participation in the European Union means that Irish laws and customs are affected by European Union laws, guidelines and decisions. The single European market has also opened up many opportunities for Irish organisations. The EU, for example, produced a directive stating that public contracts over €5 million have to be advertised across the EU. This allows Irish construction companies to compete for public contracts throughout the European Union.

2.5 The competitive environment

The performance of an organisation will be influenced by the structure of the particular industry in which it operates as this affects the level of competition in that market; for example, Mercury Engineering, Bowen Group, Jones Engineering Group, and Kirby Group Engineering (the top four mechanical and electrical companies in 2008 by turnover) are among the main competitors in this sector. Porter (1980) suggested that, to be successful, *an organisation needs to gain competitive advantage* over competitors. **Competitive advantage** means being different from or doing something better than the opposition in a way that is important to target customers.

Organisations might differentiate themselves from competitors by offering similar products at lower prices or by supplying prestige products with higher quality than the quality of opposition products.

The effective management of human resources can also be a source of competitive advantage for an organisation; for example, contented and hard-working employees are more likely to produce excellent work that adds value to their organisation. While many organisations attempt to imitate the competitive advantage of their opposition, imitating employee behaviour of opponents is, however, a difficult task. Overall, the task for managers is first to create a competitive advantage and then to sustain that advantage.

According to Barney (1996), a **sustained competitive advantage** is a competitive advantage that exists after all attempts at strategic imitation have ceased.

Porter's five forces

Michael Porter, of Harvard Business School, has taken competitive advantage as his focus in developing corporate strategy. Porter emphasises the impact of external environments on an organisation. He suggests that there are five major influences or forces which impact on an organisation's ability to compete and which determine industry profitability (see Figure 2.2):

- rivalry among existing competitors
- threat of substitute products and services
- threat of new entrants
- bargaining power of suppliers
- bargaining power of customers.

The five forces explained

1. **Competitive rivalry** is intense when there are many competitors operating in the same industry. Rivalry among competitors may appear in terms of advertising, price, quality, increased customer service, and product differentiation. An organisation needs to decide with whom it is really competing and to be aware of the main threats emerging from competitors. Competitive rivalry is intense in all sectors of the construction market with tenders for construction projects during 2009 coming in significantly under cost. Rivalry at this intense level is unsustainable, which has resulted in some companies being unable to continue to compete.

2. **The threat of substitutes** is more powerful where there are alternatives and substitutes for a company's products. Organisations, therefore, compete not only with other organisations providing similar products but also with organisations that provide substitute products. This can be a concern for suppliers operating in the built environment. Substitute materials being specified and preferred on

construction projects can lead to increased competition for suppliers; for example, uPVC window frames have replaced timber window frames, which are now viewed by some clients as obsolete.

3. **The threat of new entrants** is the extent to which new competitors can enter a market. Potential new entrants to an industry have more difficulty in setting up a high capital-intensive industry, such as a cement producing plant, than a concern that requires a smaller amount of capital, such as a small design practice or sub-contracting firm. New entrants would assess the extent of the 'barriers to entry', which might include government regulations, distribution channels and location. The threat of new entrants to the construction industry is low at present because of the current state of the market; however, during more prosperous times international construction companies, suppliers, consultancies and skilled labour entered the Irish market in significant numbers.

Figure 2.2 Porter's five forces

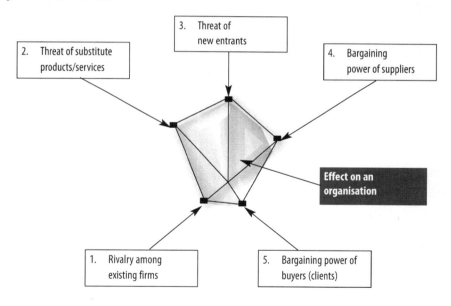

4. **The bargaining power of suppliers** depends on the availability of substitute suppliers. As a sole supplier can have great power, it is unwise for any organisation to depend on a sole supplier; a sole supplier can quite easily raise prices or reduce quality with little risk to the retention of its customer organisations. Alternatively,

where a particular organisation is the dominant customer of a supplier, that customer organisation is then in a relatively strong position, enabling it to demand lower prices, higher quality and better credit arrangements. Generally, the market for construction materials is highly competitive as there are many suppliers and the possibility of substitute products must be considered. Certain materials, however, such as crushed stone, mixed concrete, high craft-based items can often be difficult to secure locally for a project and these factors can put suppliers in a stronger position to dictate prices and terms.

5. **The bargaining power of customers** increases as customer information and advertising inform customers about the full range of price and product options available. Customers can exert pressure on organisations by demanding lower prices or higher quality. Customers have more power when they make large purchases and when alternatives can easily be found. Organisations are in a weak position if they depend on a few large customers as these customer organisations may decide to switch to competing suppliers. Clients in the built environment are buying an end product, i.e. a building, which they expect to be of high quality and standards. Currently, with competition high in the turbulent construction industry, clients and customers are putting pressure on construction companies to deliver high-quality work for lower prices.

The three generic strategies

Porter suggested that an organisation could find competitive advantage against these competitive forces through pursuing one of three **generic strategies** (see Table 2.5). Each strategy imposes different pressures on an organisation attempting to ensure that resources and capabilities are consistent with the requirements of the strategy selected. The actual choice of generic strategy depends on:
- the fit between the demands of the strategy and an organisation's capabilities and resources
- the abilities of main competitors
- the key criteria for success in a market and their match with an organisation's capabilities.

The three alternative generic strategies are:
- differentiation strategies
- cost-leadership strategies
- focus strategies.

Table 2.5 Porter's three generic strategies

Strategy	Features	Examples
1. Differentiation	Distinguishes products or services from competitors' through superior quality. Customers must value the benefits more than the extra money they have to pay.	Differentiation strategies used by: • professions—one-off house design • contractors—ISO, international standards for quality which must be met • specialists—e.g. Otis lifts • materials—steel systems.
2. Overall Cost-leadership	Operating more efficiently than competitors, thereby charging lower prices. Customers must be sensitive to price, but quality must be acceptable.	Overall cost-leadership strategy used by: • professions—budget service schedule • contractors—design and build • specialists—e.g. large-scale window manufacturers • materials—concrete systems.
3. Focus	Concentrates on a specific group of buyers, usually aimed at a limited target segment.	Focus strategy used by: • professions—regeneration design • contractors—roads and bridges • specialists—concrete bonding • materials—insulation materials.

1. A **differentiation strategy** involves an attempt to distinguish an organisation's products and services from others in the same industry segment. In order to succeed, an organisation must offer something to the customer that the customer values and which is different from the products or services of competing organisations. Product differentiation may involve branding, adding distinct features or providing extra services. If customers believe that a product is different from competitors' products they may be prepared to pay higher prices. The value added, however, must be sufficient to command a premium price for the organisation to justify the *price–value relationship*.

Builders can differentiate the houses they build by the construction methods used. Some house builders use timber frame construction to achieve high levels of thermal insulation; other builders use insulated concrete formwork (ICF) to create a robust building. All builders produce houses, but the end products are different and appeal to different clients.

2. Through the **cost-leadership strategy**, an organisation seeks a cost advantage over its competitors. This involves reducing costs in order to undercut competitors' prices while providing a product of a similar quality. The low price acts as a barrier against new entrants and substitute products. An example of a cost-leadership

strategy in the built environment is when a contractor works with a very keenly priced supplier; they can then afford to bid advantageously for projects.

3. A **focus strategy** is chosen by an organisation when it wants to be deliberately selective, focusing on a narrow group of customers rather than on the whole market. The philosophy of a focus strategy is to specialise, thus meeting the needs of a clearly defined group far better than competing organisations would. Focus in itself might not be enough, however, and an organisation may have to combine it with cost-leadership or differentiation to build competitive advantage. Focus strategies are used by construction companies who specialise in niche areas, for example retro-fitting insulation, insulated concrete formwork, quantity surveying firms who offer loan monitoring and due diligence reporting services.

Porter (1996) argued that choosing a unique position in industry is not enough to guarantee a sustainable competitive advantage, because a valuable position will attract imitating competitors. Porter believed that a manager's role is to create a fit among an organisation's activities and to integrate them so that an organisation does many things well. This requires trade-offs in competing in order to achieve a sustainable advantage, and therefore managers have to decide what *not* to do, as well as what to do.

Some managers view their organisational environment as an 'uncontrollable' element, to which they must adapt. They passively accept the environment and do not try to change it. They analyse environmental forces and design strategies that should help the organisation avoid threats and take advantage of opportunities provided by the environment.

Other managers take an **environmental management perspective**, which means that, rather than simply watching and reacting, their organisations take aggressive actions to modify environmental forces. Organisations, for example, hire lobbyists to influence legislation affecting their industries and stage media events to gain favourable press coverage. (An example of this in the built environment was the successful lobbying by timber frame manufacturers to have building regulations standards increased for thermal insulation and performance.) Managers, however, cannot always influence environmental forces; for example, it is difficult to influence geographical population shifts or the larger economic environment. Whenever possible, managers take a proactive rather than reactive approach to their environment.

2.6 Key points

The *external environment* of an organisation is composed of non-specific elements in its surroundings with which it interacts and which affect its activities. These elements include:
- social
- technological

- economic
- political–legal aspects.

The *internal* or *task environment* is composed of specific elements of an organisation's surroundings which affect its activities. These elements include:
- customers
- competitors
- suppliers
- distributors
- investors
- trade unions.

The *international dimension* is also an important element of the environment of management. The level of international business has increased in recent years. Managers need to have a clear understanding of the additional difficulties of managing internationally.

Porter suggested that an organisation's competitive environment is determined by 'five forces'. These are the:
- threat of new entrants
- bargaining power of suppliers
- bargaining power of buyers
- threat of substitute products
- rivalry among competitors.

The challenge for organisations is to achieve a competitive advantage and subsequently to sustain the advantage.

Porter also suggested that an organisation may gain its *competitive advantage* by pursuing one of three 'generic strategies':
- differentiation
- cost-leadership
- focus.

Organisations are affected by their external environment in several ways, for example changing cultural values, competitive forces and uncertainty.

Organisations use the elements of their internal environment to adapt to changes around them. The challenge for managers is to deal effectively with the constantly changing organisational environment in which they operate.

Important terms and concepts

bargaining power of customers (p. 41)
bargaining power of suppliers (p. 40)
building energy rating (p. 29)

Questions for review

1. List the forces in an organisation's external environment and discuss the impact these forces have on organisations. Illustrate your answer with an example of an organisation in the built environment sector.
2. List the forces in an organisation's internal environment and discuss the impact these forces have on organisations. Illustrate your answer in the context of an organisation the built environment sector.

3. Explain the following concepts, illustrating your answers with examples from organisations operating in the built environment:
   a. Competitive advantage
   b. Sustained competitive advantage.
4. Identify the leading professional bodies in Ireland's built environment and outline their primary roles.
5. Choose an organisation in the built environment with which you are familiar and illustrate how Porter's five forces affect that organisation.
6. Discuss the advantages and disadvantages of each of the three generic strategies for an organisation in the built environment.

3

PLANNING AND DECISION-MAKING

Learning outcomes

Following study of this chapter you will be able to:
* understand the role of planning in management
* identify individual and organisational barriers to planning
* understand the role of decision-making in management
* identify models of decision-making.

3.1 Planning defined

A plan is an explicit statement of intention that identifies both objectives and the actions needed to achieve them.

It is clear from Naylor's (2004) definition that a plan contains objectives and actions. The corporate objectives of an organisation emphasise its direct aims, which must be capable of measurement in order to confirm whether or not objectives are achieved. Organisational goals and aims are objectives that are restated in an operational and measurable form. When organisational objectives are combined with goals and aims they provide direction for an organisation. It is important that objectives are clearly expressed, realistic and have a deadline for completion. Table 3.1 highlights the criteria for successful objectives, using the SMART acronym.

Table 3.1 SMART objectives

S	Specific	Clearly and precisely expressed
M	Measurable	In order to ascertain whether or not they are achieved
A	Agreed	With those responsible for achieving them
R	Realistic	So that they can be achieved
T	Timed	With a deadline for achievement

The **action** part of the planning process clarifies the tasks required to achieve the objectives, and identifies those who are to carry out the tasks and when the actions are to be carried out. All managers plan and planning is one of the most important aspects of the management process. One of the major purposes of planning is to co-ordinate decision-making so that an organisation can move in a well-focused direction.

Without planning, the efforts of an organisation may not be well co-ordinated, and managers and employees may be heading in different directions. Planning is a very important task for managers in the built environment. A construction project needs to be carefully planned in order for it to be completed successfully. Existing projects need to be well planned, but construction companies also need to have a plan for future work, for example how to attract and bid for further projects.

Planning is also closely linked with the control function of management. Planning, for example, sets the direction for the organisation, while control ensures that the direction is maintained or, if that proves impossible, it warns of the need to choose a new direction.

The stages in the planning process are:
- formulate plans
- carry out plans
- compare outcomes with plans
- take corrective action (if necessary).

Planning has grown in importance in construction and other industries because:
- projects tend to be larger and more complex
- sub-contractors are being relied upon more
- there are greater controls over business activity, e.g. ISO (International Organisation for Standarisation) quality standards
- markets and the economy are more unstable.

Without planning, effective control of time and money is unachievable. Planning is relevant during all stages in the construction process, from inception to the design, tendering, commissioning and construction stages of a project.

Table 3.2 Examples of planning for a main contractor

Pre-Tender Planning	Pre-Contract Planning	Contract Planning
Decision to tender	Pre-contract meetings and arrangements for commencing the work	Monthly planning
Pre-tender arrangements		Weekly planning (short-term)
Site visit report		Progress reporting
Enquiries to sub-contractors and suppliers	Place subcontract orders	Report to management
Tender method statement	Site layout planning	Review/updating of health and safety plan
Build up estimate	Construction method statement	
Pre-tender programme	Master programme	
Response to pre-tender health and safety plan	Requirement schedules	
	Contract budget forecasts	
	Preparation and approval of construction health and safety plan	

Table 3.2 shows examples of good practice which would generally be put in place by larger construction organisations. At pre-tender stage the contractor will have to consider all these stages in the development of his or her estimate and the evaluation of a competitive bid. *The Code of Estimating Practice*, published by the Chartered Institute of Building, is a guide for providing estimates for building works. It covers practices from the pre-tender stage to the acceptance of a successful tender. As several decisions need to be made before the start of a project, contract planning is an essential part of a broader overall project plan. The contract plan deals with the details of work to be carried out in compliance with the overall project plan.

Reasons for *pre-tender planning* include:
- establishing a realistic contract time frame, on which the tender may be based
- identifying construction methods
- assessing items which have an impact on the bid price
- helping the build-up of contract preliminaries and plant spending
- assisting the tendering process.

Reasons for *pre-contract planning* include:
- presenting an outline plan or strategy for the project
- meeting the terms of the contract conditions
- highlighting key project dates
- identifying key information needs
- facilitating the evaluation of budgets
- planning for key dates in relation to material and sub-contractor requirements.

Reasons for *contract planning* include supervising the **master programme**. The master programme covers all the major sections of work to be carried out and clearly highlights the planned sequence of construction, making the best use of resources, monitoring the progress of the project and reporting on any variations that occur.

3.2 Levels of planning

Planning is undertaken by all managers in an organisation and is one of the core functions performed by managers. Three main levels of planning can be identified in organisations:
- strategic planning
- tactical planning
- operational planning.

Strategic plans are general plans outlining decisions regarding the allocation of resources, the priorities of an organisation and the course of action required to achieve strategic goals. These plans are set by the board of directors and top management; generally have an extended time horizon; and address questions of scope, resource deployment and competitive advantage. Strategic plans in the built environment deal with high-level selection of the overall project objectives including the project scope, procurement routes, time frame, and financing options.

Tactical plans are developed in order to implement specific parts of a strategic plan. Tactical plans specify both the resources and time available for specific projects, and generally flow from, and must be consistent with, a strategic plan. Tactical plans typically involve upper and middle management and, compared with strategic plans, have a somewhat shorter time horizon but with a more specific and concrete focus. Tactical plans, therefore, are concerned more with actually getting things done than with deciding what to do. Tactical plans in the built environment include planning the daily availability of the necessary materials, equipment and labour during the construction phase of projects.

Operational plans focus on carrying out tactical plans in order to achieve operational goals. Operational plans are concerned with turning priorities into reality and are linked to physical and human resources. They may show how many people are to be involved with a particular project, as well as the skills and qualifications of the people involved. Table 3.3 details these three planning levels. In the construction sector, operational plans provide a more detailed look at the project's resource requirements. Operational plans are developed by middle- and lower-level managers; they have a short-term focus and are relatively narrow in scope.

Table 3.3 Levels of planning in an organisation

Planning Level	Purpose	Performed By	Length of Time
Strategic	• To establish organisational objectives and goals • To match corporate objectives with available resources • To assess the external environment • To asses the internal environment	Senior management (CEO)	Long-range (3–5 years)
Tactical	• To implement specific parts of a strategic plan • To give direction and allocate resources among sub-units of departments • To focus on achievement, rather than deciding what to do	Middle management (heads of function)	Intermediate (1–5 years)
Operational	• To focus on carrying out tactical plans • To accomplish tasks with available resources • To contribute to departmental objectives	First-line management (supervisors, office managers)	Short-range (up to 1 year)

The planning process attempts to guide an organisation from its current position to where it would like to be. Effective planning is based on the co-ordination and linking of plans between the three planning levels outlined above. Most organisations use all three levels of planning to guide future actions. All levels of planning should be strongly related. Operational plans must be related to and reflect tactical plans. Similarly, tactical plans must reflect overall strategic plans. Another important element of planning is the development of contingency plans. Some of the benefits of planning in the built environment include:

1. providing management and supervisors with an effective and realistic works programme
2. assessing labour requirements
3. determining material requirements
4. facilitating the scheduling of plant and equipment
5. determining the commencement and completion of programmed activities
6. suggesting a flow of work to avoid resource imbalance
7. rearranging project priorities in the light of changed circumstances
8. preventing work overload or underload
9. providing information to head office on the progress of a project.

Contingency planning is the development of an alternative course of action to be taken if a plan is unexpectedly disrupted or becomes inappropriate. Contingency plans are efforts to cater for the 'what if' questions that emerge in dynamic environments, such as the action to be taken if a major new competitor enters the same industry sector or if there is a supply shortage. In such cases, previously made plans can be affected, and revised plans will be contingent on altered circumstances. Management, therefore, should always think through a number of options and their implications before a crisis arises.

Contingency planning is becoming increasingly important for most organisations, and particularly for those operating in complex or dynamic environments such as the built environment. Few managers have such an accurate view of the future that they can anticipate and plan for all events. Plans should therefore have a built-in flexibility, so that unexpected events such as a change in the price of raw materials can be taken into consideration. Contingency planning is a useful technique for helping managers cope with uncertainty and change. In the current economic environment, organisations should have a few different contingency plans in place to ensure that they are prepared for the unexpected.

3.3 Organisational goals

Organisations establish different kinds and levels of goals that determine organisational plans. Goals are critical to organisational effectiveness and they serve a number of purposes in the planning process. Goals, generally, have four purposes:

- to provide guidance and a unified direction for people in the organisation
- goal-setting practices strongly affect other aspects of planning, for example, setting goals and developing plans to reach them are complementary activities
- to serve as a source of motivation to employees
- to provide an effective mechanism for evaluation and control.

Goals help to shape the various levels of organisational plans discussed above. Organisational goals provide the organisation with a sense of direction. Most companies in the built environment are of a commercial nature and are motivated by economic factors such as the need to make a profit. Profit is an example of one of many goals for an organisation. According to Griffin (2008), there are generally four levels of goals in organisations:

- mission
- strategic goals
- tactical goals
- operational goals.

The **mission**, or purpose, is the organisation's reason for being. Pearce and David (1987) define an organisation's mission as:

> A statement of its fundamental, unique purpose that sets a business apart from other firms of its type and identifies the scope of the business's operations in product and market terms.

The mission is the foundation for all subsequent plans in an organisation. A **mission statement** is a statement of an organisation's purpose. Mission statements vary in length, complexity, detail and philosophy. Most mission statements tend to be generalised, but they provide a sense of direction to guide more detailed planning and strategy formulation. Mission statements usually contain *vision* (the desired future of an organisation) and *strategic intentions* (main activities, the desired position, and the support and constraints in achieving these activities).

Roadstone, for example, one of Ireland's leading manufacturers and suppliers of building materials, has the following mission statement (www.roadstone.ie):

> Our vision is to continue to be the leading supplier of building materials in Ireland. We will achieve this by securing adequate reserves which will be extracted and further processed using proper plant and equipment in a safe, healthy and environmentally compliant way. Our priority is to give a superior service to our customers. Management asks all employees and contractors to be totally committed to this objective. We will stick to our core business and produce and supply quality products giving excellent value to our customers whilst making maximum use of modern technology. The development of new

products, markets and systems of operation is critical to the progress of the company and employees are invited to share their ideas with management. We will be a responsible neighbour in the communities in which we operate and deliver on our social responsibilities, especially the health and safety of all. We must be a vibrant and learning organisation with a healthy mix of depth of skills and backgrounds supported by on-going training. We are committed to supporting our parent company, CRH plc, and to enhancing shareholder value.

Michael Punch and Partners Ltd, one of Ireland's leading consulting engineering firms specialising in civil, structural and environmental engineering, has the following mission statement (www.mpp.ie):

By fostering, developing and maintaining our human and technical resources, we deliver to our clients a standard of service that makes our company name synonymous with all that is excellent in structural, civil and environmental engineering.

It is clear from their mission statements that these organisations concentrate on quality when dealing with suppliers, staff and customers.

Successful organisations operate according to their mission statements by ensuring that employees are aware of the mission statement in order to successfully implement its values. Mission statements, objectives and goals bring many benefits, including:

- *unity of direction*—aiming for a co-ordinated effort (rather than individual efforts) by employees in achieving organisational objectives and goals
- *motivation*—offering individuals a sense of personal achievement in the process of achieving objectives, and committing them to their organisation
- *basis of control*—providing criteria for measuring desired and actual outcomes from objectives denoting the performance that is expected of employees.

Strategic goals are set by organisations' top management (for example, the board of directors, chief executive officers, managing directors). These goals focus on broad issues and have a long-term time frame, typically three to five years. An architectural practice, for example, may have a ten-year strategic objective to become the leading practice in architectural conservation in a particular geographical area.

Tactical goals are set by middle management. These goals focus on the actions necessary to achieve the broader strategic goals and have a medium-term time frame of one to five years. An architectural practice, for example, may have a two-year goal to train all design staff in architectural conservation.

Operational goals are set by lower-level managers. These goals focus on issues associated with tactical goals and have a short-term time frame, usually less than one year, but they can run for just weeks or days. The design leaders in an architectural practice, for example, may have quarterly goals for their design staff to achieve prescribed skills in architectural conservation.

3.4 Barriers to planning

Planning can be obstructed by both individual and organisational barriers.

Individual barriers to planning include:

- managers who believe that planning is unnecessary or a waste of time
- managers who are more concerned with solving day-to-day matters than with planning for the future
- managers who view planning as a threat
- managers who do not wish to commit themselves to specific planning objectives
- resistance to change (generally part of planning), because of fear of the unknown among managers and employees
- lack of clarity about the purpose of the planning process among employees who have been promoted to operational managerial positions and who have not received adequate training in planning
- a construction manager tendering for a project who is not confident of winning the tender and may not commit to planning at this stage.

Organisational barriers to planning include:

- inadequate support for planning from top management
- plans that are too abstract to be translated into operational plans
- a dynamic and complex environment resulting in rapid change, which militates against the proper assessment of future long-term opportunities and threats (for example, because of rapidly changing technological environments)
- an excessive emphasis on planning which may lead to over-sophisticated plans which may not be easily implemented
- use of sophisticated programming software, such as Microsoft Project and Primavera, which may result in plans becoming too complex and causing difficulties in implementation plans during the construction stage.

Overcoming barriers to planning

1. **Understanding the purpose of plans**. Managers should recognise the basic purpose of planning and understand that well-executed plans will lead to more effective and efficient organisations.
2. **Communication and consultation**. Plans must be communicated to all employees in an organisation through proper communication channels (rather than through the grapevine or gossip). Managers and employees responsible for achieving organisational goals should be consulted to ensure a sense of 'ownership' of the plans.

3. **Training**. Appropriate training in planning skills will reduce insecurity and uncertainty and help plans to be implemented effectively.
4. **Top management support**. Top managers need to be actively involved and educated to see the benefits of planning in order to help middle-level and lower-level managers recognise top management's view of planning as an important managerial function.
5. **Developing plans with clear objectives and goals**. Plans should not be too abstract, but should have easily identifiable targets which all employees should readily understand.

3.5 Planning in practice: management by objectives

In 1954, Peter Drucker first proposed **management by objectives (MBO)** as a method of implementing strategic objectives. MBO attempts to integrate individual and organisational objectives. The responsibilities of each employee are specified in terms of measurable results so that they can be used by employees in planning work. The MBO philosophy promotes employee participation when setting objectives as this strengthens the motivation to achieve the objectives. The results can be monitored by employees as well as managers. MBO provides a method of involving all employees and focusing individual objectives to be integrated into a strategic plan.

A primary step in MBO is the communication, by managers to employees, of organisational goals and plans that have been established. Goals are then specified for accomplishment in particular time frames. Plans developed to achieve particular goals are stated clearly and linked directly to each goal. In order to facilitate the achievement of both personal and organisational goals and plans, managers, in conjunction with employees, must first ensure that the goals that are set *are* attainable.

MBO allows the review and adjustment of previously set objectives in order for them to remain relevant and achievable, and feedback can be used for employees' personal development and be built into employee performance appraisal, which is conducted regularly (often annually) by many organisations. The advantages of MBO are recognised in terms of individual improvements on past performance, particularly where individual employees determine their own objectives and where there is feedback on performance. MBO is traditionally used in the built environment for project appraisal. Appraisals are normally undertaken separately on construction projects, by measuring the progress of a task or element against its objectives. MBO is the most common method of evaluation in the built environment.

3.6 Decision-making

Decision-making means choosing one option from a number of options: that is, options have to be identified and the 'best' option chosen. The decision-making process, therefore, includes recognising and defining the nature of a decision situation, identifying alternatives, selecting the 'best' choice and putting it into practice. Decision-making is closely linked to the planning process because managers who are developing and implementing plans, at all levels, have to make decisions on organisational strategies. Decisions can be divided into three main categories:

- strategic
- administrative
- operational.

Strategic decisions are concerned with the achievement of long-term corporate plans and organisational objectives. These decisions are made by top management, often after lengthy consideration of all related factors, because the decisions may have major consequences for the future of an organisation. Strategic decisions in the built environment include:

- expansion into different areas of construction work
- developing policies to deal with sub-contracting work and employing direct labour
- dealing with international competition
- forming strategic alliances
- merger or company takeover
- contracts bidding.

Strategic decisions are typically related to one-off (rather than ongoing or routine) situations where each individual situation is considered and evaluated as it arises. Senior managers should reconsider objectives and take into account new techniques to ensure the company's future survival. Strategic decisions in the built environment relate to project stages including pre-design, design, tender, construction, occupancy, maintenance and disposal and differ in nature. These decisions tend to be complex, made in conditions of uncertainty and have a long-term impact on project success.

Administrative decisions follow on from strategic decisions and are concerned with establishing ways of implementing procedures and systems so that an organisation can operate in an effective and efficient manner.

Administrative decisions also support operational decisions (see below). Examples of administrative decisions for a construction company include procedures governing:

- payroll
- contracting suppliers and distributors
- decisions on human resource procedures
- estimating practices during the competitive bidding process for contractors.

Though they are relatively infrequently required, administrative decisions are usually made by middle managers.

Operational decisions are day-to-day procedural decisions that have to be made on an ongoing basis. Operational decisions are made by front-line managers (or supervisors) and operate in the short term. Managers making operational decisions are helped by procedures that have been previously put in place, for example standard guidelines for scheduling and co-ordinating sub-contractors. Site managers work mainly at an operational level. Examples of operational decisions for a construction company include:

* reordering office supplies
* calculating holiday pay
* dealing with routine demands
* customer complaints
* pricing
* site planning
* departmental budgets
* project budgets.

Managers making operational decisions are helped by procedures that have previously been put in place, for example standard guidelines for reordering supplies or for dealing with complaints made by customers.

3.7 Models of decision-making

Two well-recognised models of decision-making are the *classical* model and the *administrative* model.

The **classical model** guides managers on how they should make decisions. The classical model emphasises the making of decisions in a rational and logical manner, and assumes that:

* Decision-makers seek full information on practically all options before making a choice.
* Objectives are clear and agreed.
* Problems are clearly defined.
* Decision-makers can eliminate situations of uncertainty to achieve a condition of certainty for any decision.
* Decision-makers evaluate all aspects of a decision situation logically and rationally.

There are, however, some problems associated with the classical model and, indeed, management theorists have concluded that managers are often unable to make rational decisions because of the following.

* The classical model sets out how decisions should be made, but does not describe how managers make decisions in practice.

- Problems are usually ill-defined.
- Objectives are often unclear.
- It is almost impossible to consider all other options.
- Very few conditions of real certainty exist.
- Decision-makers may not evaluate all situations rationally and logically but may be influenced by political, social and cultural norms.
- Decisions made by managers at the outset of a construction project will be heavily influenced by government planning policies and procedures.

Decision-makers may make decisions based merely on intuition or on a hunch, therefore not making the 'logical' decision that the classical model requires.

Herbert A. Simon recognised that decisions are not always made with rationality and logic, and his **administrative model** describes his view of how decisions are often *actually* made, in contrast to prescribing how decisions *should* be made. The administrative model recognises that:

- objectives are often unclear and may not have been agreed
- problems may not have been clearly specified
- decision-makers' searches for options are limited
- decision criteria may not have been established in advance.

Decision-makers, faced with these problems, often have incomplete and imperfect information on which to base their decisions, for example a quantity surveyor may not have a full copy of the drawings or specifications when measuring the quantities of materials for inclusion in a bill of quantities. A **bill of quantities** is a document used in tendering in the construction industry in which components of a building are described and quantified and their prices determined. It also ideally details the terms and conditions of the construction or repair contract and itemises all work to enable a contractor to price the work for which he or she is bidding. Bills of quantities are prepared by quantity surveyors based on estimates from drawings and specifications in an architect's drawings. These are used to create a cost estimate in regard to the square area in metres of walls and roofs, the numbers of doors and windows, and systems such as heating, plumbing and electrics.

Bounded rationality means that people set limits on how rational they can be. The boundary may arise from previous experiences of decision-making, skills and habits. While organisations and their environments become more and more complex and unclear, people are only able to process a limited amount of the available information. An experienced site manager may have developed skills and habits over many years of site work; however, if they are moved to a project that uses a radically new construction method, they may have difficulties in dealing with such new procedures because they might not have had the opportunity to upskill or re-skill. Retraining and the provision of time for the development of new decision-making and problem-solving skills may be required for the site manager to operate effectively in such a changed project environment.

Satisficing means choosing the first option that meets the minimum decision criteria rather than conducting an exhaustive search for the best possible option. Decision-makers tend to satisfice because of the problems associated with collecting, memorising, comprehending and communicating vast amounts of information. Members of a construction project team may occasionally have to satisfice because of time and costs constraints. A client, for example, may ask for a certain type of cladding to a building, but if the option is too expensive and does not fit into the budget, the client and team members will have to satisfice to reach an appropriate solution.

In summary, the classical model is prescriptive as it explains how decision-makers might attempt to be more rational and logical in their approach to decisions. On the other hand, the administrative model can be used by decision-makers to develop a better understanding of the limitations in the decision-making process.

3.8 The decision-making process

In attempting to make good decisions, managers generally go through various procedural steps (outlined in Figure 3.1).

Figure 3.1 The decision-making process

STEP 1	Recognising and identifying the decision situation
STEP 2	Identifying options
STEP 3	Evaluating options
STEP 4	Choosing options
STEP 5	Implementing chosen options
STEP 6	Following up and evaluating results

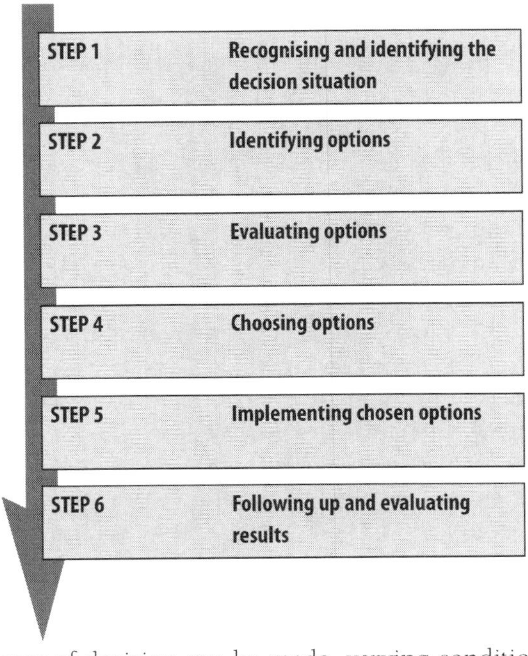

Just as different types of decision can be made, varying conditions exist in which managers have to make decisions.

- *Certainty*—where managers make decisions in circumstances of certainty, the available options and conditions associated with each option are known to be certain. Very few decisions, however, are made with certainty because of the turbulent environment in which organisations operate.

• *Risk* —where managers make decisions under risk, the available options are known, but their outcomes are doubtful.

• *Uncertainty*—where managers make decisions with uncertainty, only some of the available options and their associated risks are known. In the current economic climate, an increasing number of decisions are made with uncertainty. Managers need to have good intuition and judgment.

• *Recognising and identifying the decision situation*—acknowledging the reason for a decision: the reason may be positive or negative. In many negative situations there are no prior warnings, for example in the case of mechanical failure. Once the decision recognition phase has occurred, a manager has to ensure that a clear definition of the opportunity or problem is provided.

• *Identifying options*—managers should try to identify as many options as possible in order to reach the 'best' decision. Managers may be constrained by financial, legal, economic, and political forces in identifying options.

• *Evaluating options*—having identified a number of options, managers can evaluate each identified option. Options are evaluated on a number of criteria, such as feasibility, projected satisfactory outcome, financial implications, and the manner in which each option fits with overall organisational objectives. A site manager, for example, may have to evaluate the available options based on his or her knowledge of the local situation even though the senior manager, who may have more experience, is located at head office, which may be far from the site.

• *Implementing chosen options*—after an option has been decided on, it can be implemented. The successful implementation of any option usually requires managers to communicate the basis for their decision to employees, so that employees can understand the decision and give their commitment to implementing the particular option chosen. A site manager, for example, may postpone the excavation of a deep foundation if weather forecasts predict exceptionally inclement weather. Explaining this to construction employees should enable them to appreciate why alternative work has been allocated and may dispel fears of the project being abandoned.

• *Following up and evaluating results*—after the decision has been implemented, managers need to evaluate the results and provide feedback to employees. Evaluation helps managers assess whether the decision has been effective, and also helps with future decision-making. Following the excavation of a deep foundation once weather conditions have improved, the site manager should assess the original decision to postpone the work in comparison to the actual performance achieved following this decision. This will measure the value of the decision and should improve future planning and decision-making for the site manager.

3.9 Group decision-making

In many organisations, decisions are made by groups rather than by individuals. In some situations groups will provide the best decisions and in other situations individuals will be better. Group decision-making is widely used in the built environment. Project teams comprising various professionals from different disciplines, for example architect, quantity surveyor, structural engineer and services engineer, are set up at the beginning of a project. Each professional brings a different set of skills to the group, which assists in decision-making and problem-solving over the course of the project. Table 3.4 summarises the advantages and disadvantages of group decision-making.

Table 3.4 Advantages and disadvantages of group decision-making

Advantages	Disadvantages
• More information and knowledge become available. A team of design professionals can produce a more comprehensive design solution than an individual designer.	• Group decisions take longer and increase costs. Very large design teams can take a considerable length of time to resolve design issues to each design member's satisfaction.
• The number of possible options is likely to be increased. Awareness of the full range of construction procurement routes can enable the most suitable procurement route to be selected for a construction project.	• Groups can be indecisive and may satisfice rather than seeking all the available options. The temporary nature of a construction team may limit the nature of interaction between group members.
• The involvement of more people should increase the likelihood that the decision will be accepted. Recommendations from the entire design team on the best design solution for a client should make it easier for the client to accept the recommendation.	• Groups may be dominated by an individual with a strong personality. Design team members are often under time pressure to deliver a completed design and can be pressurised into making hasty design decisions.
• Better communication of a decision should result. A design team can present a design in a variety of ways to help people understand the design concept, for example drawings, scaled models, animated software simulations, detailed cost reports, and structural calculations.	• Groupthink may occur (where a group wishes to reach a decision without reaching the best possible decision).

3.10 Key points

The *planning process* is an essential managerial function for organisations, where managers develop different types of goals and plans. To serve a variety of purposes, organisations develop various goals, for example:

- mission
- strategic goals
- tactical goals
- operational goals.

Organisational goals help managers develop organisational plans. The main types of plan are:

- *Strategic*—set by top management, addressing long-term issues for an entire organisation.
- *Tactical*—in operation at the middle level of an organisation, developed in order to implement specific parts of a strategic plan, having an intermediate time frame.
- *Operational*—implemented at the lower level of an organisation, with a short time frame, aimed at achieving operational goals.

Individual and organisational barriers to planning may exist despite the benefits of planning, which should be obvious to managers. Managers have to develop a number of strategies to successfully overcome these barriers. An example of planning in practice is MBO, which attempts to integrate individual and organisational objectives in an overall strategic plan.

Decisions, even if usually associated with the planning process, are a core part of all managerial activities. *Decision-making* is the act of choosing one option from a number of options. Decisions are made under conditions of certainty, risk or uncertainty. Decisions can be made by individuals or groups: there are both advantages and disadvantages to each option. Two recognised models of decision-making are the classical model and the administrative model.

The *classical model* assumes that managers have complete information and that they will behave rationally. The *administrative model* recognises that managers do not always have complete information; they may not always act rationally; and they may satisfice.

Important terms and concepts

administrative decisions (p. 56)
administrative decision-making model (p. 58)
barriers to planning (p. 54)
basis of control (p. 53)
bill of quantities (p. 58)
bounded rationality (p. 58)
certainty (p. 59)

classical decision-making model (p. 57)
code of estimating practice (p. 49)
contingency planning (p. 51)
decision-making (p. 55)
decision-making process (p. 59)
group decision-making (p. 61)
ISO quality standards (p. 48)
levels of planning (p. 49)
management by objectives (p. 55)
master programme (p. 49)
mission (p. 52)
mission statement (p. 52)
models of decision-making (p. 57)
motivation (p. 53)
operational decisions (p. 57)
operational goals (p. 53)
operational plans (p. 50)
overcoming barriers to planning (p. 54)
planning (p. 47)
risk (p. 60)
satisficing (p. 59)
SMART objectives (p. 47)
strategic decisions (p. 56)
strategic goals (p. 53)
strategic plans (p. 49)
tactical goals (p. 53)
tactical plans (p. 50)
uncertainty (p. 60)
unity of direction (p. 53)

Questions for review

1. Explain the purposes of planning for an organisation operating in the built environment.
2. Describe the barriers to effective planning and suggest how these barriers might be overcome.
3. Distinguish between strategic, tactical, operational and contingency planning, giving an example for each of an organisation operating in the built environment.
4. Describe the steps in the decision-making process. Illustrate each step with an example of the process relating to an organisation operating in the built environment.

5. Distinguish between strategic, administrative and operational decisions in terms of organisations operating in the built environment.
6. Compare and contrast the classical and administrative models of decision-making.

4

LEADING AND LEADERSHIP

Learning outcomes

Following study of this chapter you will be able to:
- describe leadership
- trace the development of leadership theories
- understand different theories of leadership
- identify the relationship between leadership styles and management.

4.1 Leadership defined

> Leadership is the process of motivating people to act in particular ways in order to achieve specific goals.

Naylor's (2004) definition indicates clearly that leadership is an ongoing process which involves the motivation of others to achieve the common goals of an organisation. Authority and responsibility are essential components of leadership in deciding the way forward and in the success or failure of achieving agreed goals. Leadership provides inspiration and guidance through interaction with others to achieve certain ends. It also involves **power**, which is usually defined as *the potential to influence the behaviour of others*. According to Hannagan (2008), if leadership is seen as a process and as a series of actions which can be identified, it can be learned, to some extent. In recent years, the word 'vision' has become closely associated with leaders and leadership. Vision, in essence, is what an organisation wants to become.

4.2 Theories of leadership

Leadership has been a subject of investigation for centuries, but it is only since the 1950s that theories of leadership have emerged. Various theories have been put forward, from the traditional view that leaders are born, not made, to the more recent view that leadership depends on particular situations rather than on a particular set of universally shared traits. In an effort to recognise the 'exceptional characteristics' that leaders possess, one of the earliest theories of leadership concentrated on identifying leadership traits.

Trait theories

Trait theories concentrated on the *qualities* required for effective leaders, suggesting that leaders are born, not made. Trait theorists sought to identify particular personality traits which were common to all leaders and which caused them to be self-selected leaders. The traits or characteristics that appeared most frequently were:

- intelligence
- height (that is, physically tall)
- energy
- initiative
- maturity
- vision.

Despite various studies of leadership, however, no common characteristics have emerged. Research has found that particular traits or characteristics, which separate leaders from non-leaders, cannot be identified—contrary to the view that leaders are born and not made. It is now recognised that certain traits increase the likelihood that a leader will be effective, but they do not guarantee effectiveness, and the relative importance of different traits is dependent upon the nature of the leadership situation.

Michigan studies

Researchers at the University of Michigan, USA, led by Rensis Likert, studied leadership during the 1940s and reported their findings in 1950. These studies were based on interviews with leaders (managers) and followers (employees). The results of the interviews produced the **Michigan continuum**, which suggests that leaders are either people-focused or task-focused (Figure 4.1).

Figure 4.1 The Michigan continuum

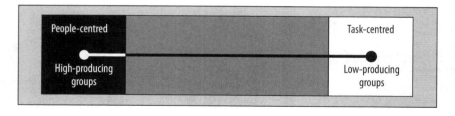

People-focused managers:
- pay close attention to the work relationships of their employees
- encourage employee participation in decision-making
- strive for job satisfaction for their employees.

Task-focused managers, at the other end of the continuum:

- are more directive
- pay close attention to explaining work procedures clearly
- are interested in performance.

Likert argued that people-focused leaders tend to be more effective, as his studies showed that managers who are people-focused are high-producing leaders. Managers who are task-focused tend to be less productive. The Michigan studies also found that people-focused leader behaviour tended to be organic and flexible, whereas task-focused leader behaviour tended to be rigid and bureaucratic. Leaders, however, may have a style which lies somewhere in between the two and it should be noted that Likert studied only the two end styles for contrast. Construction managers cannot afford to overlook either people or task issues. This suggests that, in the built environment, combining elements of people-centred and task-centred leadership may be most effective.

Ohio State studies

During the late 1940s, researchers at Ohio State University in the USA also identified two styles of leadership. Their studies were based on extensive questionnaire surveys and produced results similar to the findings of the Michigan studies. The terms used by the researchers at Ohio State University were *consideration* and *initiating structure*.

Consideration leadership has an *informal* approach to management which:

- considers employees' feelings
- focuses on employees' well-being
- provides feedback to employees
- encourages the participation of all employees through two-way dialogue and communication
- promotes a 'good' working environment for managers and employees.

This behaviour involves a leader's concern for improving communication and developing mutual trust and liking between the leader and employees. The Ohio State studies viewed **consideration** as behaviour indicative of friendship, mutual trust, respect, and warmth in the relationship between the leader and the members of his or her staff.

The **initiating-structure** leadership style defines clearly who the leader is, has a *formal* management approach and focuses on issues such as:

- planning
- organising
- controlling
- allocating tasks
- work processes in general.

Initiating structure involves a leader clearly indicating the relationship between himself or herself and members of the organisation, and endeavouring to establish well-defined channels of communication and methods of procedures throughout the organisation.

The major difference between the Ohio State studies and the Michigan studies is that the Ohio researchers believed that it was possible for leaders to practise both consideration *and* initiating-structure styles of leadership. The Ohio State researchers, for example, showed that it was possible for a manager to score high on consideration and also on initiating structure.

In summary, leadership which is high on both initiating structure and consideration behaviours tends to be the most effective form of leadership. It would appear that there is no one best way of leadership. A leadership approach, however, that is suited to controlling sub-contractors may not be effective on site for direct labour.

Leadership grid

An extension of the Ohio State studies was the *leadership* or *management grid*. The **leadership grid** (Figure 4.2) provides a means of evaluating leadership styles. Introduced by Blake and Mouton in 1962, it suggests that leadership behaviour is multidimensional insofar as leaders can exhibit a number of behaviours that interact with each other. Blake and Mouton suggested 81 possible interactions, but defining each of these positions was not practical, so five extreme positions were described. The horizontal axis represents *concern for production* (similar to task-centred and initiating-structure behaviour) and the vertical axis represents *concern for people* (similar to employee-centred and consideration behaviour).

Figure 4.2 Blake and Mouton's leadership/managerial grid

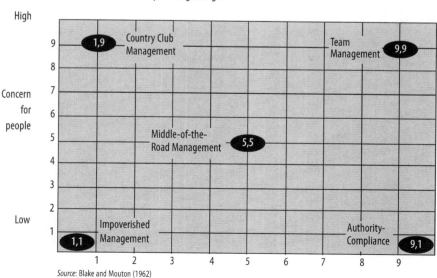

Source: Blake and Mouton (1962)

Blake and Mouton defined *concern for production* as concern with whatever an organisation seeks to achieve. *Concern for people* refers to a leader's attention to the people who are engaged with achieving organisational goals. This concern includes building organisational commitment and trust, promoting personal worth of employees, providing proper working conditions and rewards, and promoting good interpersonal relations.

The five positions identified in the grid are:

- *Impoverished management* (score 1,1 on the grid)—low concern for both employees and production. Managers operating an impoverished management style avoid responsibility and contact with employees, and rely on previous practice to run an organisation.
- *Authoritarian management* (score 9,1 on the grid)—high levels of concern for production and efficiency and low levels of concern for employees. As this management style is task-oriented, managers believe that their responsibility is to plan, direct and control their employees. Authoritarian managers also believe that employees are a commodity just like machines and enforce their own decisions over the wishes of their employees. On a construction site, a leader may assume an authoritarian management style when faced with a task-related problem which needs an immediate decision. An authoritarian management style may be used, for example, if concrete has arrived on site and is ready to be poured. Steel reinforcement bars may have just been fixed in position. A decision needs to be made immediately in relation to whether the steel reinforcement bars have been fixed correctly and whether the formwork has not been disturbed. The site engineer does not have time to discuss the problem with others. At this point he or she has to become task-orientated.
- *Middle-of-the-road management* (score 5,5 on the grid)—unlikely to involve managers who are dynamic leaders. Middle-of-the-road managers believe in compromise, whereby they get acceptable levels of production but also have concern for employees. These managers have confidence in their employees and make decisions only when endorsed by their employees.
- *Country club management* (score 1,9 on the grid)—high emphasis on concern for people and low emphasis on concern for production. Employees working with this style of leadership report high levels of satisfaction as they are encouraged and supported by their managers, and employees tend to work in harmony.
- *Team management* (score 9,9 on the grid)—high on concern for both employees and production. Managers operating the team management style believe that concern for employees and concern for tasks are compatible. These managers aim at combining the highest possible standard of production with all employees agreeing on a high level of commitment in order to achieve the best possible results for all stakeholders. Blake and Mouton argued that this management style provides the most effective leadership as it fosters long-term development and teamwork.

Contingency approaches to leadership

Contingency approaches to leadership assume that appropriate leader behaviour depends on situational variables. Different situations demand different kinds of leadership, requiring individual leaders to adapt styles to the requirements of different situations.

Tannenbaum and Schmidt's contingency theory

Research on effective leadership styles have shown that these depend on many variables, such as:

* management style
* individual personality
* the culture in the organisation
* the tasks to be performed.

The contingency approach suggests that there is no leadership style that is effective in all situations. In 1958, Robert Tannenbaum and Warner Schmidt developed a **leadership continuum** (see Figure 4.3), which suggested that various factors influence the choice of leadership styles. They concluded that there are three main factors or 'forces' from which a leadership style is developed:

* *Personal forces*, such as the personal background of managers, their confidence and experience. Different managers will have different skills and experiences.
* *Characteristics of subordinates*, such as a manager's need to consider the willingness or unwillingness of subordinates to accept responsibility and to make decisions. On construction sites, the structure of groups can change regularly. Groups will aim to balance task requirements with their own needs.
* *The situation itself*, which suggests that managers need to recognise the situation in which they find themselves, in the context of their corporate culture, colleagues' work style, and the time limit and nature of the tasks to be performed. Construction work tends to be repetitive, which suggests the need for stringent controls. Other tasks, however, may be one-off and left to the resourcefulness and judgment of the leader involved.

Common to all contingency approaches is the requirement for leaders to behave in a flexible manner, and to have the ability to diagnose and apply the leadership style appropriate to any particular situation. The continuum identifies extremes in leadership styles: for example, at one end is the autocratic leader (using what Tannenbaum and Schmidt term 'boss-centred leadership') who makes all decisions alone; at the other end are employees having complete freedom to make decisions with minimal guidance (which they term 'subordinate-centred leadership'). Between these two extremes, according to Tannenbaum and Schmidt, there are a number of points on the continuum that influence leadership style, and each point is influenced by the three forces identified (personal forces, characteristics of subordinates, the situation itself).

In suggesting that leaders might vary their styles, Tannenbaum and Schmidt viewed leadership as something that could be learned from experience. They challenged the belief that either directive (autocratic) or participative (democratic) leadership was superior. They contended, for example, that a directive leader is better when time is scarce or when circumstances are difficult, such as in a crisis situation; in contrast, participative leadership is more appropriate where experienced subordinates can exercise good decision-making skills.

Figure 4.3 Tannenbaum and Schmidt's leadership continuum

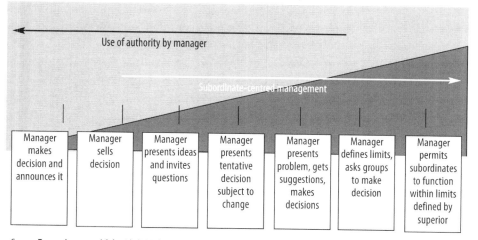

Source: Tannenbaum and Schmidt (1958)

Overall, the leadership continuum suggests that leadership style shifts the focus from the individual manager in isolation to the manager in the context of the combined tasks to be performed and the characteristics of the subordinates. Table 4.1 looks at two typical styles of leadership in the context of a construction project.

Table 4.1 Tannenbaum and Schmidt continuum applied to a construction project

Leadership Factors Normally Required	Design Team with Architect as Leader	Brickwork Gang with Trade Foreman as Leader
Personal forces	Creative, experienced, design-focused, good people skills.	Disciplined, job-focused, strong man management skills.
Characteristics of subordinates	Professional, self-motivated, require chairmanship ability and long-term planning skills.	Accurate direction and short-term planning from leader.
The situation itself	Challenging but favourable working environment.	Difficult physical working environment.
Most suitable leadership style (based on Tannenbaum & Schmidt continuum)	Subordinate-centred.	Boss-centred.

Fiedler's contingency theory

Fiedler developed his **leadership contingency model** in 1967. This model suggests that the appropriate style of leadership varies with the favourableness of the situation. Fiedler believed that the performance of employees is contingent on a leader adopting an appropriate style, depending on whether the situation is favourable or unfavourable. If the task is misunderstood or the construction manager is unpopular or lacks authority, a firm stand is required to take control. Fiedler suggested that the three most important variables in determining the relative favourableness of a situation are:

- *Leader–member relations*—the relationship between a leader and employees in regard to issues such as trust, respect and confidence in each other. Good relations foster the effectiveness of a leader.
- *Degree of structure in task*—the defining of tasks for employees. A task is structured when it is routine, unambiguous and easily understood. An unstructured task is non-routine and complex. A structured task is more favourable for a leader as employees will know what to do, without major guidance from a leader.
- *Power and authority of the position*—if the leader has power and authority to act on each situation, power is assumed to be strong. Alternatively, if a leader has to seek approval from others, power is assumed to be weak. From the leader's point of view, the position of strong power and authority is more favourable.

From these three variables, Fiedler suggested that leaders are either *task-oriented* (similar to initiating-structure behaviour) or *relationship-oriented* (similar to people-focused or consideration behaviour). Fiedler suggested that the most favourable situation for leaders to influence their group was one in which they have good leader–member relations, hold high-position power, and are directing a high task structure. In contrast, a most unfavourable situation for leaders is where they are disliked, have little position power, and face an unstructured task. From questionnaires, Fiedler developed an instrument called the **least-preferred co-worker (LPC)** to classify these two leadership styles. The measuring scale asks leaders to describe people with whom they have worked and to think of the one with whom they worked least well. The leader is given a set of sixteen scales, and the leader's LPC is calculated by totalling the numbers marked on each scale. Figure 4.4 illustrates two of the sixteen scales.

Fiedler suggested that a high total score reflects a relationship-oriented leader, but that relationship-motivated leaders will score relationship issues high despite their problems with the LPC. A low score reflects a task-oriented leader, but rates the LPC low on all dimensions. Fiedler believed that both these leadership styles are effective, depending on the situation involved.

Fiedler suggested that task-motivated leaders have low LPC scores: they focus on details; and will be tough and autocratic on any uncommitted subordinates in

Figure 4.4 The least-preferred co-worker theory of leadership

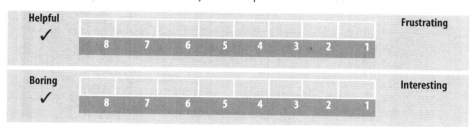

order to complete a task. Their self-esteem comes from completing tasks. They are only considerate when tasks are going well.

Productivity holds the higher value for these leaders. Relation-motivated leaders have high LPC scores, get bored with details, and focus instead on pleasing others, getting loyalty and being accepted. Their self-esteem comes from interpersonal relationships. In the built environment, the design team leader is often required to be a motivated leader in order to manage and lead the team of professionals within the design group. In the harsh environment of the construction site the trade foreman is often required to adopt a more task-oriented approach to ensure tasks are completed to the required quality and on schedule.

Vroom-Yetton-Jago contingency theory

Victor Vroom, Philip Yetton and Arthur Jago based their model of leadership style on the decision-making practices of managers. This model is narrower than other contingency theories insofar as it focuses on one part of the leadership process, that is, the amount of decision-making participation that, ideally, should be granted to employees. The model was first proposed by Vroom and Yetton in 1973 and was revised and expanded by Vroom and Jago in 1988. They suggested that decisions are generally characterised by three variables:

- the quality of the decision (the effect of the decision on performance)
- acceptance of the decision by employees (the extent to which employees are committed to the decision)
- the time needed for the decision to be made.

The Vroom-Yetton-Jago model outlines decision styles which range from the purely autocratic (AI) at one end to total participation style (G) at the opposite end.

The Vroom-Yetton-Jago contingency theory suggests that, depending on these three variables, it is possible for leaders to select a decision style. Their theories proposed five main decision styles for leaders that depend on the degree of participation by employees in the decision-making process:

- *Autocratic I (AI)* —managers make the decisions themselves using available information.
- *Autocratic II (AII)*—managers obtain information from employees regarding the decisions to be made but make the decisions themselves.

- *Consultative I (CI)*—managers obtain and share information regarding decisions to be made with employees individually but the managers make the decisions themselves and these may or may not be influenced by the opinions of employees.
- *Consultative II (CII)*—managers share the decisions to be made with employees as a group and obtain their ideas and information, but the managers may or may not use the ideas generated when making decisions.
- *Group participation (G)*—managers share the decisions to be made with employees as a group, which allows for managers and employees to consider various solutions; managers act as co-ordinators in order to reach an agreement, which might then be implemented.

The Vroom-Yetton-Jago model suggests that leaders might choose between different styles depending on the particular decision-making circumstances. This contrasts with the views of Tannenbaum and Schmidt, who believed that different leaders have different styles, but will consistently follow their own particular style.

Path-goal theory

The path-goal theory was proposed by Martin Evans and Robert House and is associated with the motivation of employees (see Chapter 7). The path-goal theory suggests that leaders can influence employees by recognising and satisfying their expectations. The theory also suggests that leaders can make valued or desired rewards available and ensure that employees understand the behaviour which should lead to those rewards. The path-goal theory suggests that leaders should motivate employees (through support, direction, guidance and training) and clarify the paths for employees to attain their goals. According to the path-goal theory there are two main variables which influence leadership style:
- Personal characteristics, which include factors such as:
  - ability
  - skills
  - motivation.
- Workplace characteristics, which include factors such as:
  - rules governing authority and responsibility
  - the clarity of a task to be executed.

Path-goal theory, therefore, is concerned with a leader clarifying the path and adjusting the goals to help employees accomplish their goals and receive valued rewards. The path-goal theory identifies four kinds of leader behaviour:
- *Directive leadership*—managers tell employees what they have to do, let employees know what is expected of them and give guidance and direction.
- *Supportive leadership*—managers adopt a friendly and approachable style, display concern for the welfare of employees and treat employees as equals.
- *Participative leadership*—managers consult employees, take their opinions into account and allow participation in decision-making.

- *Achievement-oriented leadership*—managers set clear and challenging goals, encourage employees and expect them to perform at high levels.

In summary, the path-goal theory assumes that managers can change leadership styles in order to meet the demands of particular situations. Personal characteristics and workplace characteristics are recognised as the two key variables that define the behaviour of leaders, and this in turn can influence the behaviour of employees.

From the above theories, it is clear that leadership is a social process that involves interaction with others. In a constantly changing social, economic, and technological environment, leadership has become more important than it was in the past. One of the main challenges to a project leader in the built environment is to ensure that the tasks of all individuals on the project team are planned, co-ordinated, managed, monitored, and controlled in order that the project is completed on time, within budget, and is of high quality.

In summary, an examination of recent leadership literature shows that prevailing leadership thinking is dominated by *contingency* theory. Contingency theory holds that leadership has to continually adapt in order to respond to ongoing changing contexts. As organisations are continually changing, this implies that leadership also has to change continually, since leadership has to respond to new and unique sets of circumstances on a daily basis.

Transformational leadership

Transformational leadership is one of the most topical approaches in leadership studies since the early 1980s. Transformational leadership is a process that is meant to transform individuals. It assesses followers' motives, endeavours to satisfy their needs, and respects their dignity as human beings. Transformational leaders are seen as visionaries who challenge people to achieve high standards in everything they do. Transformational leadership is a process that includes:
- charismatic leadership (sharing complete faith in a leader)
- inspirational motivation/leadership (communicating high performance expectations)
- intellectual stimulation (enabling others to think about old problems in new ways)
- individualised consideration (actively giving personal attention to all individuals).

Changes in the marketplace and workforce in the last quarter of the twentieth century resulted in the need for leaders to become more transformational and less transactional, if they are to remain effective. **Transactional leadership** is viewed as manipulative, using continual bargaining to determine what employees need to do to achieve personal and organisational objectives. In contrast, **transformational**

leaders motivate followers to achieve more than they would have expected by raising motivation and the importance of the value of individuals' tasks within an organisation. Transformational leaders go beyond transactional leadership by using the power of their own vision and energy in order to inspire their employees.

One of the main characteristics of transformational leadership is charisma. Charismatic leadership in the built environment is generally observed on high-profile projects. Construction project team members from different organisations are more likely to respond to transformational leadership. During times of change and economic unrest, transformational leadership is highly valued in all organisations.

It is important to recognise that management and leadership, although related, are different. Management is broader in scope; for example, management is concerned with choosing goals, solving problems and identifying developments in the environment. Leadership involves risk-taking and motivating and inspiring people to achieve goals. In summary, leadership determines *where* an organisation is going and influences people in particular directions, whereas management describes *how* the organisation can get there.

According to Senge (1990), 'leadership is a phenomenon, not a position'. It is not determined by hierarchy, as leaders can emerge from teams of middle management. Senge suggests that leaders are people who move ahead and who have some influence over others. Capowski (1994) suggests that management and leadership differ in that one comes from the head and the other from the heart. The manager is associated with qualities that come from the head:

- rationality
- tough-mindedness
- authority
- analysis
- structure
- persistence
- problem-solving
- stabilising.

The leader, on the other hand, is associated with qualities that come from the heart:

- creativity
- flexibility
- inspiring others
- innovativeness
- courage
- imagination
- vision
- initiating change.

Kotter (1986) made a more detailed distinction. He saw management as predominantly *activity*-based, whereas leadership means dealing with people rather than things. Currently there is a great deal of emphasis on developing leadership in those with responsibilities for managing people. Effective leadership has become one of the current management issues in organisations. There is a particular emphasis on transformational or visionary leadership and the ability to inspire others through instilling in them the purpose and mission of the organisation.

In practice, however, the most effective managers are also leaders and the quality of leadership has become an increasingly important part of management ability. Organisations need both management and leadership in order to successfully achieve organisational goals.

4.3 Leadership style in the built environment

In the built environment, there are a number of factors which have an impact on the leadership style during construction projects. These include:

- client characteristics
- project characteristics
- contractual arrangement.

Client characteristics

The client characteristics will be different for each project and will depend on whether the client is from the public or private sector. The private sector client will generally emphasise quality and time. Private clients require the building or development to be of a high standard so that it can be sold or let. In addition to emphasising quality and time, the public sector client is more likely to emphasise the importance of keeping the project within budget. These factors will influence the client's choice of contractual arrangement and the type of leadership to be expected on site.

Project characteristics

All projects vary in size and complexity. Different styles of leadership are needed to increase the probability of success of a building project. A participative style of leadership may be more appropriate than a directive style for a large and complex project, as it will take longer to build. Leadership style on construction sites will also be influenced by the nature of the tasks involved. Unstructured and irregular tasks with undefined goals and objectives will require a more directive and tight style of leadership than structured and regular tasks.

Contractual arrangement

Another factor that influences leadership style is the choice of procurement route. The most common procurement routes in Ireland are:

- traditional contracting
- management contracting
- design and build
- project management.

The main influence that the choice of procurement route has on the style of leadership is the ratio of sub-contracting to direct labour used on construction sites. Each contractual arrangement presents different conditions to be adhered to throughout a project and the leadership style needs to be able to adapt to manage the project and deal with any risks which may be transferred to the different parties. In 2007, the Department of Finance issued an edict that in future all government-funded infrastructural projects should be procured under a new form of contract called the GCCC Form of Contract. These new contracts have given rise to debate in relation to the transfer of risk from the employer to the contractor during the project (See Chapter 10).

4.4 Key points

Various theories of leadership (summarised in Table 4.2) have emerged during the past century. The *trait approach* to leadership was one of the first studies conducted with the aim of identifying important leadership traits. The trait approach initially assumed that some common traits separated leaders from non-leaders. The results of the research, however, suggested that there were no traits common to all leaders.

Subsequent research at the University of Michigan and Ohio State University identified two basic forms of leadership behaviour: one concentrated on *work* and the *tasks* to be performed; the other focused on employee *welfare* and support for employees. Another approach to leadership is shown in the *leadership grid*, which identifies wide variations in leadership and management styles.

Contingency approaches to leadership recognise that the behaviour of leaders is not universally applicable to all situations; rather, a particular situation dictates the behaviour of leaders. Fiedler's leadership contingency model, for example, suggested that the style of leadership varies depending on a particular situation or context.

The *leadership continuum*, developed by Tannenbaum and Schmidt, suggests that leaders are at either end of a continuum, that is, they are either boss-centred or subordinate-centred. Similarly, the LPC (least-preferred co-worker) scale suggests that a leader's behaviour should be either task- or relationship-oriented, depending on the particular situation.

The *path-goal theory* suggests that a leader's behaviour may be supportive of employees or it may be achievement-oriented, depending on the personal characteristics of employees and on the environment. The *Vroom-Yetton-Jago model* suggests that leaders should vary the extent to which they allow employees to participate in decision-making. The leadership theories outlined above illustrate that management and leadership are related, but they are not the same. In practice, in an era in which the quality of leadership in organisations plays an increasingly important role, the most effective managers are also leaders.

Table 4.2 Summary of leadership theories

Theory	Characteristics
Trait theory	Attempted to identify traits common to all leaders.
Michigan studies	Leaders are either people-focused or task-focused.
Ohio State studies	Leadership style uses either initiating-structure or consideration behaviour.
Leadership grid	Leadership is multidimensional, a mix of concern for production and for people.
Tannenbaum and Schmidt	Leadership continuum suggesting that leaders are either boss-centred or subordinate-centred.
Fiedler	Style of leadership varies between task and relationship orientation, depending on situation.
Vroom-Yetton-Jago model	Leadership style is based on decision-making practices of managers.
Path-goal theory	A leader's primary functions are to make desired rewards available to employees and to clarify for employees the behaviour that will lead to those rewards.
Transformational leadership	Leaders are seen as visionaries who challenge people to achieve high standards in everything they do.

Important terms and concepts

charismatic leadership (p. 75)
client characteristics (p. 77)
contractual arrangements (p. 78)
Fiedler's contingency theory (p. 72)
leadership defined (p. 65)
leadership grid (p. 68)
least-preferred co-worker (LPC) (p. 72)
Michigan continuum (p. 66)
Michigan studies (p. 66)
Ohio State studies (p. 67)
path-goal theory (p. 74)
power (p. 65)
project characteristics (p. 77)
relationship orientation (p. 72)
Tannenbaum and Schmidt's leadership continuum (p. 70)
task orientation (p. 72)

trait theories (p. 66)
transactional leadership (p. 75)
transformational leadership (p. 75)
Vroom-Yetton-Jago contingency theory (p. 73)

Questions for review

1. Discuss the dimensions of leadership with reference to the Ohio State studies, the Michigan studies and the leadership grid.
2. Should the circumstances in which leadership is exercised make a difference to the style of leadership? Discuss using examples from the built environment.
3. Write brief notes on:
   a. Fiedler's leadership contingency model
   b. the Vroom-Yetton-Jago contingency theory
   c. the path-goal theory.
4. Analyse the main considerations leaders should take into account when making decisions, using examples from a construction project to illustrate your answer.
5. Why should the leadership style be different in a design team situation and in a work crew situation on a construction site?

5

ORGANISING AND CONTROLLING

Learning outcomes

Following study of this chapter you will be able to:

- understand what is meant by organising (in management)
- understand the traditional organisational structure for a construction project
- recognise the link between organising and organisational structure
- explain the nature of control in organisations
- understand the purpose of control in an organisational context
- identify various types of organisational control.

5.1 Organising defined

> Organising is the arrangement of all elements of an organisation to achieve its strategic objectives.

From this definition (Naylor 2004), we can see that organising is concerned with activities such as deciding and choosing the best way to group organisational resources. Organising is the process of designing jobs, grouping jobs into manageable units, and establishing patterns of authority between jobs and units. Organising and planning are closely linked. Plans state the direction and intentions that managers have for an organisation (see Chapter 3) and organising is the process of co-ordinating individuals and groups in an organisation for the purpose of executing the plans in the most efficient and effective manner in order to achieve organisational goals. The framework used for organising is **organisational structure** (see 5.4 Organisational structures).

Organising can represent a complex process for the construction industry as it is a highly fragmented industry. For a construction project to be completed, a client will normally appoint a design team consisting of professionals from different firms, for example an architect, structural engineer, quantity surveyor, mechanical and electrical engineers. More complex projects will require additional construction professionals (for example a planning consultant). While the design team or organisation works on behalf of the client, each professional works within the hierarchy of their own firm and would typically be involved in a number of construction projects at any one time. Similarly, the construction process, which follows the design stage, will require a main contractor to organise a project structure of many sub-contractors to get the building constructed. These temporary, or project, organisational structures require careful planning and management for both design teams and contractors but can yield efficient and cost-effective solutions for clients requiring new buildings.

5.2 Traditional organisational structure for a construction project

The traditional organisational structure for a construction project, also known as the traditional procurement system, involves the appointment of independent consultants to act on behalf of the client to produce the design and supervise the construction. A main contractor is employed to construct the building. The architect nominates specialist sub-contractors called *nominated sub-contractors* to work with the main contractor. The main contractor can also appoint sub-contractors of his or her own, called *domestic sub-contractors*. Project delivery is viewed as a sequential process with design being largely completed before the employment of the contractor.

Figure 5.1 Traditional organisational structure for a construction project

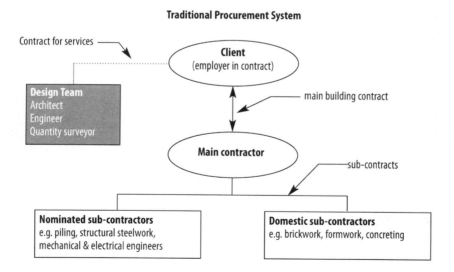

The traditional procurement system (Figure 5.1) is the most frequently used system for small to medium-sized projects in Ireland. It is well known and understood by consultants and contractors. A range of standard documents such as contracts, specifications and methods of measurement (bills of quantities) have been developed for the traditional system. This system is regarded as a good method for achieving high quality at a reasonable cost and with reasonable speed in the building process. It also has the advantage of being able to accommodate client modifications during construction.

As the building process is becoming more complex, with additional new regulations and planning considerations, many clients now employ a project manager or personal adviser to act and advise on their behalf with design teams, contractors, local authorities, etc.

5.3 Organising employees

The division of labour in an organisation is the manner in which employees are organised or divided so that different tasks can be performed by different people. **Job specialisation** is an example of the division of labour whereby employees become specialised in specific but limited tasks. The rationale for job specialisation is that it should:

* lead to a more efficient use of labour
* develop employee expertise through repetition of a task
* reduce times for completing tasks as a result of familiarity.

The increasing use of sub-contracting within the construction industry is an example of job specialisation. Sub-contractors are now organised by technical capability or trade, for example brickwork, steel fixing, glazing, electrical, etc.; however, job specialisation has associated disadvantages, such as boredom and dissatisfaction, and its inherent lack of challenge or stimulation can contribute to a rise in absenteeism. Construction work can be physical in nature and consequently can lead to occupational injury when it is allowed to become highly repetitive—bricklayers, for example, can suffer from repetitive strain injuries when continuously laying heavy concrete blocks. Concreting crews can suffer from *white knuckle*, a condition associated with using vibrating equipment over extended time periods.

In order to counteract the problems associated with job specialisation, other techniques for the division of labour are often introduced:

* **Job rotation** involves moving employees from one task to another in a systematic way. Employees tend to be more satisfied at first, but satisfaction tends to wane because jobs deemed suitable for rotation tend to be fairly routine.
* **Job enlargement** can be introduced to increase the total number of tasks performed by employees to counteract employee dissatisfaction and lack of motivation which occurs when the same task is repeated. Job enlargement, however, increases training costs and in many instances the tasks remain routine and boring.
* **Job enrichment** increases both the number of tasks an employee performs and

the amount of control an employee has in performing tasks. This can be effective as employees who are granted more authority assume a sense of responsibility for the tasks they perform.

- **Work teams** enable employees to decide how tasks will be allocated; they monitor their own progress as a team and have autonomy over the scheduling of tasks.

5.4 Organisational structures

An organisation's structure has been defined by Mintzberg (1979) as:

> the sum total of the ways in which it divides its labour into distinct tasks and then achieves co-ordination between them.

The structure of an organisation refers to:
- the size of its hierarchy
- its spans of control
- its division of labour
- its means of co-ordination.

As noted in Chapter 1, **hierarchy** is associated with bureaucratic types of organisation, where there are many layers of management grades between senior managers and junior employees. **Span of control** refers to the number of employees reporting to a particular supervisor or manager. A narrow span of control means that a small number of employees report to a manager, whereas a wide span means that a large number of employees report to a manager (see Figure 5.2).

Figure 5.2 Narrow versus wide spans of control

Closely related to the span of control is the **division of labour**. Organisations with wide spans of control and relatively few levels of management grades are called *flat structures*, whereas organisations with narrow spans of control with many managerial levels are called *tall structures* (see Figure 5.3). Mintzberg suggested that the span of control and division of labour depend on the type of task to be performed, whether direct supervision is needed or not, and on the experience of managers and employees. The span of control can be influenced by different factors. The distance between a manager and the team they are supervising can reduce the span of control. A sub-contracting company, for example, may have several work teams operating on various projects in different locations. Full-time supervision will not be required for each of the work teams so the span of control is reduced.

Figure 5.3 Tall versus flat organisational structures

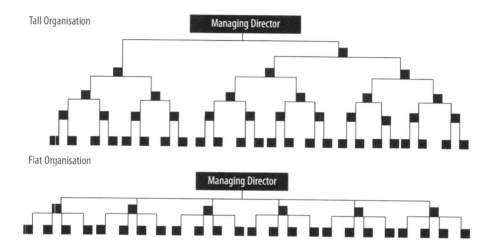

As construction companies attempt to decide whether to use directly employed labour or sub-contracted labour they will take into account the different spans of control associated with each option. Generally, directly employed labour will work well under a wide span of control as they will have a long-term relationship with the contractor, their direct employer. Using sub-contracted labour creates a greater risk for the contractor as these employees will not be well known to the contractor, therefore a narrow span of control will generally be used. The increased cost of this narrow span of control, which requires greater site supervision than directly employed labour, is normally offset by the lower sub-contracting costs of the labour.

A final element in determining organisational structure is the **co-ordinating activity**. Many organisations break down the tasks to be performed and co-ordinate these by grouping similar activities together and by forming departments, for example production, marketing, finance and human resources departments. This is known as **functional departmentalisation** (see Figure 5.4). After departments have been formed, however, the activities of departments must be linked to ensure that all departments are focused on achieving common organisational goals. The co-ordinating activity provides the link between departments because each department depends on the other to perform their respective activities.

Figure 5.4 Functional organisational structure for a medium-sized construction company

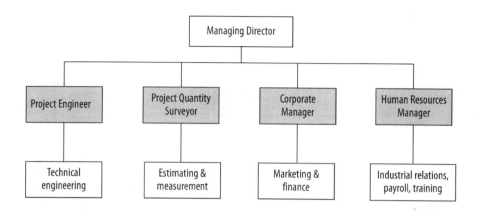

Product departmentalisation is another method of co-ordinating activities. This means grouping tasks associated with particular products. Many large organisations that produce a number of products or services divide their activities into business units, with each unit responsible for its own product. Each business unit would have its own set of resources and its own specialist employees. The co-ordinating activity must ensure that each business unit does not focus exclusively on its own product, but that it contributes to the overall goals of the organisation. Figure 5.5 illustrates product departmentalisation in relation to a construction company operating in the built environment:

Figure 5.5 Organisation structure by project departmentalisation

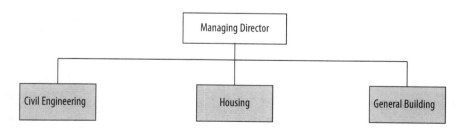

In recent years, many construction companies have moved from product departmentalisation to structuring the company under different procurement methods. Figure 5.6 highlights this type of structure.

1. *Public–private partnership (PPP)* is a procurement method where a building project is operated and funded through a partnership consisting of a public authority with a private construction company.
2. *Design and build* is a procurement method whereby the contractor is responsible for the design, management and delivery of the project, on time and within budget.
3. The *traditional* procurement method is where the majority of the work is designed by the client and the construction work is undertaken by the contractor.

Figure 5.6 Organisation structure by procurement route

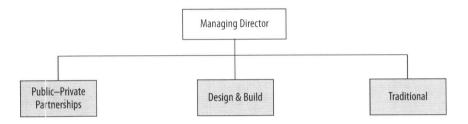

Organising based on procurement systems enables specialist knowledge and personnel to be developed with high levels of skill and experience in delivery of specific projects. Each of the three procurement systems identified in Figure 5.6 can represent separate business units within the overall business model of a firm. Cost and profit centres can demonstrate the performance of each sub-structure within the organisation and can enable management to be guided by procurement in the business strategy of the firm.

A third method of co-ordinating activities is **customer departmentalisation**, which means arranging tasks to respond to and interact with specific customers and their needs. Customer departmentalisation can increase responsiveness to customer needs and can use skilled specialists to deal with individual market segments. Many construction design and consultancy firms appoint experienced personnel to head up client centres within their organisation. Typically this may be based on:

- **public sector client:**
  - health
  - education
  - infrastructure
  - public buildings
- **private sector client:**
  - retail
  - hotel

- medical
- industrial
- pharmaceutical.

Geographical, or **location**, **departmentalisation** occurs when an organisation structures its activities in various geographical locations. Geographical departmentalisation is suitable for organisations operating in many different countries as it enables organisations to respond to local markets. Geographical departmentalisation, however, requires a large number of managers who can focus on local issues rather than on broader organisational goals. One example is Kentz, which had its origins in Ireland and is now a global engineering and construction specialist with over ten thousand employees operating in twenty-six countries world-wide.

5.5 Delegation, decentralisation and centralisation

Another important element of organisational structure is the determination of how authority is to be distributed among positions. **Authority** is power that has been legitimised by the organisation. Specific issues that managers must address when distributing authority include delegation, decentralisation and centralisation.

Delegation

Delegation is the process by which a manager assigns a portion of his or her total workload to others. The delegation process involves three steps.
1. The manager assigns responsibility, or gives the subordinate a job to do.
2. Along with the assignment, the individual is also given the authority to do the job.
3. The manager establishes the subordinate's accountability, that is, the subordinate accepts an obligation to carry out the task assigned by the manager.

Decentralisation

Just as authority can be delegated from one individual to another, organisations also develop patterns of authority across a wide variety of positions and departments. These processes are known as decentralisation and centralisation. Managers in all organisations have to decide on how much authority to delegate from the top. Griffin (2008) defines **decentralisation** as *the process of systematically delegating power and authority throughout the organisation to middle- and lower-level managers*. Table 5.1 shows two types of decentralisation that can be used by companies in the built environment.

Table 5.1 Decentralisation in a construction company

Type of Decentralisation	Used by a Construction Company
Regional Decentralisation	When a construction company is working on various projects in different locations. Regional decentralisation will help the company cope with the local conditions affecting each project.
Product Decentralisation	When a construction company works on various different types of project, for example hospitals, factories and domestic housing. Organisational efficiency can be improved through product decentralisation.

Some advantages of decentralisation:

- Decision-making processes are accelerated as managers do not have to continually refer to top management.
- Motivation is increased as middle and junior managers are given additional responsibilities.
- Top managers can concentrate on strategic issues of their organisation.

Some disadvantages of decentralisation:

- Managers may place excessive emphasis on their own particular issues rather than working for the interests of the total organisation.
- Customer service can become inconsistent, particularly in service industries (for example, architecture, engineering, quantity surveying).
- There may not be an adequate communication system in place to prevent errors.

Overall, most commentators suggest that the advantages of decentralisation outweigh the disadvantages.

Centralisation

Centralisation has been defined by Griffin (2008) as *the process of systematically retaining power and authority in the hands of higher-level managers*. In centralised organisations, decisions and responsibility for the whole organisation are retained by top managers.

Some advantages of centralisation:

- It is possible to have a common policy for the whole organisation.
- Conflict between middle- and lower-level managers can be prevented.
- Co-ordination and control of the whole organisation is easier to achieve.

Some disadvantages associated with centralisation:

- Control and authority may be excessive.
- Common policies may not be appropriate throughout the whole organisation.
- Motivation may be inhibited.
- Initiative may be stifled.

No organisation is ever completely decentralised or completely centralised. There are a number of factors which determine its position. These include:

- *The external environment*—the greater the complexity and uncertainty of the environment, the greater the tendency to decentralise.
- *History of the organisation*—organisations have a tendency to do what they have done in the past, in terms of decentralisation or centralisation.
- *Nature of the decisions being made*—the costlier and riskier the decision, the more pressure there is to centralise.
- *Ability of lower-level managers*—if lower-level managers have talent and ability, there is likely to be a high level of decentralisation.

5.6 Line and staff

Organising differentiates between *line* and *staff* functions and relationships. A **line function** contributes *directly* to the achievement of an organisation's primary goals. 'Operating manager' is an increasingly popular term for someone previously called a line manager. Typical line employees are involved with production and sales. With line relationships, formal authority is created by the organisational hierarchy, for example by production managers exercising authority over production staff. A quantity surveyor operating in a professional quantity surveying practice has a line function with the senior quantity surveyor from whom he or she takes instructions.

A **staff function** contributes indirectly to an organisation by supporting line functions and relationships. Staff functions provide expertise and advice, including engineering, surveying, commercial, legal and human resources support for line managers. Staff authority is often exercised through managers having the authority to offer advice/instruction in relation to specialist functions or standards in an organisation. Commercial directors and human resources directors, for example, while having responsibility for their respective specialist functions, have the authority to insist that line managers and employees adhere to the organisation's policies in relation to these financial and human resource functions. An estimator in a construction company will have a staff function with the company's site manager.

Today, however, many organisations have blurred this distinction. New forms of organisation design and a trend toward smaller staff units, for example, have shifted traditional work arrangements. As a result, although human resource activities are still seen as staff functions, line managers often have responsibility devolved to them for carrying out some human resource management functions.

5.7 Control

As discussed in Chapter 1, control is one of the basic functions of management. Control is the regulation of organisational activities in order to achieve organisational objectives and goals. Control keeps an organisation moving in the right direction by measuring actual performance against desired performance. Control can include taking corrective action when needed so that an organisation may reach its targets.

The control function is closely linked to the planning and organising functions, as control aims to keep an organisation on an intended course. Without the control function, organisations have no indication of how well they perform in relation to their goals. At any point in time, the control function will compare where the organisation is in terms of performance (financial, productive or otherwise) to where it is supposed to be. Control provides an organisation with a mechanism for adjusting its course if performance falls outside acceptable boundaries.

Control on a construction project aims to manage the requirements to meet time, cost and quality outcomes. These factors put the project under tension and frequently pull the project in the direction of a greater force, for example to lower costs or to reduce time (see Figure 5.7).

Figure 5.7 A construction project under tension

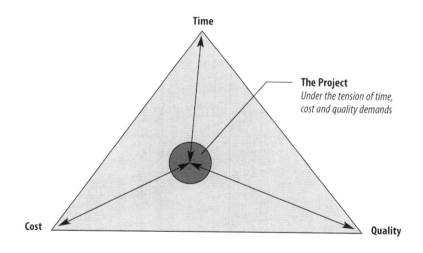

The control process

The control process has four fundamental steps (see Figure 5.8).

1. **Establishing standards of performance**. A *control standard* is a target against which subsequent performance will be measured. Standards of performance need to be realistic and clearly stated, for example in units of production:
   • square metres of walling per day
   • cubic metres of concrete per day.
   Control standards should also be consistent with organisational goals (see Table 5.2).

2. **Measuring performance**. The next step in the control process is to measure performance. The measurement of performance depends on the adequacy, relevance and validity of information generated in an organisation. Organisations may measure performance on a daily, weekly or monthly basis; for example, building contractors use daily work returns to measure sub-contractor and worker performance. Monthly progress statements are submitted to clients for cash flow payments (see Table 5.2).

3. **Comparing actual results against standards**. The third step in the control process is comparing actual results against established standards. Actual results may be higher than the standard, some may be identical and some may be lower. If the actual results are far lower than the standard, organisations may need to review their goals and take corrective action to improve performance. Large construction companies use cost variance analysis to measure deviations between planned expenditure and actual expenditure during the construction process. Negative deviations result in corrective actions to mitigate against further financial losses and to improve standards and methods of construction.

4. **Determining the need for corrective action**. This is the final step in the control process. If the actual results are far lower than the desired standard, managers may introduce appropriate action to increase performance or they may change the standard. Control, therefore, involves identifying progress and correcting actions to improve overall organisational performance.

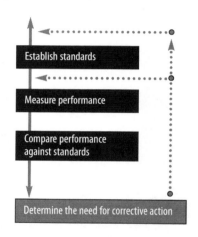

Figure 5.8 The control process

In terms of progress, the contractor should be particularly concerned with controlling the elements listed in Table 5.2.

Table 5.2 Controlling standards in the construction process

Control Objectives	Monitoring (Historical)	Controlling (Future)
Production – quality & quantity	Quantity and quality of physical construction work being achieved.	Changes required to the quantity and quality of physical construction work required to meet future standards.
Production – sub-contracting	Effectiveness of domestic and nominated sub-contractors on site.	Changes required to domestic and nominated sub-contractors' performance on site.

Production – programme	Is the programme being achieved?	How will the programme be achieved?
Contractual	Impact of variations and contract positions thus far.	Anticipated variations and contract positions and their effect on the construction process.
Information	Is the flow of design information allowing for the planning and organisation of the construction work?	What information flows will be required to allow planning and organising future work?
Financial	Cash flow analysis should allow the contractor to evaluate the cost of materials purchased, the cost of labour, the cost of preliminaries (management costs) and the rate of progress payments from the employer.	The contractor also needs to know the future cash flow position based on past and current progress.

Types of control

Many methods of control are used by organisations. The two main classifications of control are financial and non-financial.

Financial control

Financial control is the control of financial resources as they flow into and out of an organisation. The most commonly used methods of financial control used in organisations are:

- budgetary control
- break-even analysis
- ratio analysis
- financial audits.

BUDGETARY CONTROL

A budget may be defined as *a plan expressed in numerical terms* (Needles *et al.* 1999). The usual time period for a budget is generally one financial year, i.e. 1 January to 31 December. Building projects typically lasting two to three years, including the design stage, are commonly budgeted for on a monthly basis. Building contracts provide for interim valuations for contractors on either a monthly or a milestone basis. The milestone periods are not defined in terms of time but rather in terms of the completion of defined elements of work, for example sub-structure, superstructure, etc. The contractor is paid once a milestone has been achieved, therefore the sooner the milestone is completed, the quicker and more positive cash flow becomes.

A budget is an action plan for the immediate future of an organisation. Budgetary control takes the targets of desired performance as its standards, then produces information in relation to actual performance and identifies the differences between the desired and actual performance.

Budgets generally use financial data, but they may also be expressed in terms of units of production or sales volume (e.g. housing units). Budgets enable performance to be measured across departments, through various hierarchical levels in an organisation, and from one period to another. Budgets may be further subdivided into *financial*, *operating*, and *non-monetary*, as illustrated in Table 5.3.

Table 5.3 Types of budget

Budget Type	What Each Budget Illustrates
Financial budget:	
cash budget	Cash income and cash expenditure
capital expenditure budget	Costs of major assets, for example, new building, machinery
balance sheet budget	Forecast of an organisation's assets and liabilities
Operating budget:	
sales budget	An organisation's income from its activities
expense budget	Projected expenses for an organisation
profit budget	Projected differences between sales and expenses
Non-monetary budget:	
labour budget	Number of employee hours available for use
production budget	Number of units to be produced
space budget	Floor space available for various departments or functions

Generally, the main aims of budgetary control are to:
• establish short-term business plans
• assess progress in achieving short-term plans
• ensure co-ordination between various departments in an organisation.

Information provided from various sources, for example sales, production, capital expenditure and cash, are gathered to form a master budget, which is a statement of budgeted profit and loss together with a projected balance sheet. In the built environment, construction projects will have their own individual budgets. Construction companies will have different budgets relating to different departments, such as estimating, plant and equipment, and administration.

BREAK-EVEN ANALYSIS

The second financial control is called break-even analysis. This involves the use of fixed and variable costs to analyse the break-even point at which it becomes profitable to produce a good or service. *Fixed costs* (also known as *overheads*) are costs that do not vary with production or sales levels. Regardless of production output, for example, an organisation must pay bills for rent, power, interest and salaries. Fixed costs occur regardless of variable costs. *Variable costs* vary directly with levels of production. They are called variable because their total varies with the number of units produced. *Total costs* are the sum of the fixed and variable costs for any given level of production (see Figure 5.9).

Figure 5.9 Break-even chart for an architectural practice

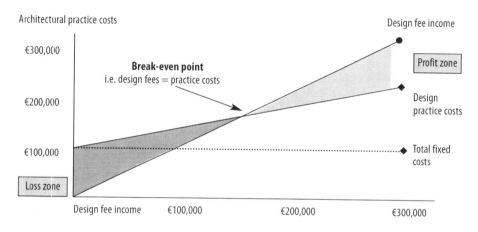

When managers analyse the level of both fixed and variable costs, they can identify the income needed to break even, and this information can be made available on a break-even chart (see, for example, Figure 5.9). This break-even chart illustrates how costs and profits vary with the level of design services and fee income for an architectural practice. The break-even point on the chart is where the total costs line crosses the design fee income line and that is the point where neither a profit or loss is made.

Overall, break-even charts indicate the effects on profits of marginal changes in revenue (e.g. fee income) or in costs. The charts provide a graphic illustration of how much fee income should be generated before profits can be made. The straight lines on the charts, however, may be over-simplistic, therefore break-even analysis should be used in tandem with other control mechanisms for greater accuracy.

RATIO ANALYSIS

Another aspect of financial control is the analysis of performance data. A *ratio* provides a useful tool for this type of analysis. Financial ratios are relationships that exist between accounting figures, and are usually expressed in percentage terms. Ratio analysis allows an organisation to monitor its performance over time and to compare it with competitor performance. Some examples of financial ratios include:

$$\text{Net profit margin} = \frac{\text{Net profit}}{\text{Sales}} \times 100$$

$$\text{Current ratio (liquidity)} = \frac{\text{Current assets}}{\text{Current liabilities}}$$

Ratios can provide useful information regarding the progress or efficiency of an organisation, particularly when comparisons are made with competitors. As with break-even analysis, ratios should be used in conjunction with other methods of performance analysis.

FINANCIAL AUDITS

Financial audits are independent appraisals of an organisation's accounting, financial and operational systems. The two major types of financial audit are the external audit and the internal audit.

External audits are financial appraisals conducted by experts who are not employees of the organisation. External audits are typically concerned with ensuring that the organisation's accounting procedures and financial statements are compiled in an objective and verifiable fashion. The organisation contracts certified public accountants for this service.

Internal audits are handled by employees of the organisation. Their objective is the same as that of an external audit—to verify the accuracy of financial and accounting procedures used by the organisation. Internal audits also examine the efficiency and appropriateness of financial and accounting procedures.

Non-financial controls

In addition to financial control, organisations may also utilise a number of non-financial control mechanisms.

QUALITY CONTROL

The role of quality control is to ensure that appropriate standards of quality are set and that deviations from particular standards are rejected. Quality control is therefore a system for setting quality standards, measuring performance against those standards and taking appropriate action to deal with any deviations from those standards.

Many building contractors and design and construction consultancy firms in Ireland have successfully implemented the International Organisation for Standardisation's quality scheme, ISO 9000. This is a quality management system which focuses on the needs of the customer. Several firms have also acquired the ISO 1400 quality programme, which focuses on environmental management.

INVENTORY CONTROL ON CONSTRUCTION SITES

The construction process uses a wide variety of materials on site, ranging from live/short-life materials such as ready mixed concretes and mortars to long-life durable materials such as pre-cast concrete. To maintain effective inventory control of materials on site, the purchasing function must connect the demand for materials on site with the installation of materials on site. Any errors in lead times can be expensive. Effective systems such as the just in time (JIT) approach can contribute to cash flow savings but require careful planning and purchasing. Similarly, purchasing must meet all specification requirements for the achievement of quality standards.

5.8 Managing control in organisations

For control systems to be effective in organisations, they need to be:
- *linked with planning*—for example, when goals are set, control mechanisms should be an integral part of planning to achieve goals.
- *flexible*—for example, inventory control must be capable of accommodating changes in quantities of raw materials.
- *objective*—for example, the control system should provide information that is as objective as possible for managers.
- *timely*—for example, when information is needed for control purposes, it must be available as often as is necessary.

Managers should realise that employees may resist control, particularly if they believe they are over-controlled. The extent of resistance depends on the balance of the control system, its design and the manner and the circumstances in which control is implemented. Mullins (2007) proposes that resistance to control will be greater when the control system:
- measures performance in a new area
- replaces a system that people have an interest in retaining
- uses standards that are set without participation
- does not feed results to those whose performance is measured
- feeds results to higher levels in an organisation
- provides results to be used by the reward system
- affects people who are satisfied with the way things are and who regard themselves as committed to an organisation's aims
- affects people who have low self-esteem.

Managers, however, can help overcome resistance to control by encouraging employee participation in planning and in implementing the control system. The control function is often controversial because the benefits of control systems are not always obvious to employees. Managers should ensure that employees recognise that control mechanisms are effective, properly integrated with organisational planning, flexible, accurate, timely and objective. The successful implementation of a control process is vital for the effective completion of a construction project. Construction projects are becoming more complex in scale and size, and due to advances in technology, such as more complex software or plant (which calls for employees to be trained in these new operations), there is increased need for effective control of projects and employees.

5.9 Key points

Organisational structure refers to the division of employees and of tasks. Employees may be organised in various ways, for example according to:
• job specialisation
• job rotation
• job enlargement
• job enrichment
• work teams.

Organisational tasks may be organised through:
• functional departmentalisation
• product departmentalisation
• customer departmentalisation
• geographical departmentalisation.

Organisations develop patterns of distributing authority across a wide variety of departments and positions. This distribution of authority can be thought of as a continuum with *decentralisation* at one end and *centralisation* at the other. No organisation is completely decentralised or centralised.

The managerial function of *control* is closely linked to the functions of planning and organising. Financial and non-financial control is concerned with regulating organisational activities to minimise errors and to achieve organisational goals more efficiently and effectively. The *control process* consists of four steps:
• establishing standards of performance
• measuring performance
• comparing actual results against standards
• determining the need for corrective action.

Employees may resist control if they perceive that they are being over-controlled. Managers can overcome this resistance by improving the effectiveness of controls and by increasing employee participation in developing control processes.

Important terms and concepts

authority (p. 88)
break-even analysis (p. 94)
budgetary control (p. 93)
centralisation (p. 89)
control (p. 90)

control process (p. 91)
customer departmentalisation (p. 87)
decentralisation (p. 88)
delegation (p. 88)
design and build (p. 87)
design team (p. 81)
domestic sub-contractor (p. 82)
financial audit (p. 96)
financial control (p. 93)
flat structure (p. 84)
functional departmentalisation (p. 85)
geographical departmentalisation (p. 88)
interim valuations (p. 93)
inventory control (p. 96)
ISO 1400 (p. 96)
ISO 9000 (p. 96)
job enlargement (p. 83)
job enrichment (p. 83)
job rotation (p. 83)
job specialisation (p. 83)
line and staff (p. 90)
nominated sub-contractor (p. 82)
organisational structure (p. 84)
product departmentalisation (p. 86)
public--private partnership (p. 87)
quality control (p. 96)
ratio analysis (p. 95)
tall structure (p. 84)
traditional procurement system (p. 82)
work teams (p. 84)

Questions for review

1. Why is organising a complex process in the construction industry?
2. Describe the traditional organisational structure for a construction project.
3. Write brief notes on:
   a. job rotation
   b. job enlargement
   c. job enrichment.
   d. work teams.
4. Explain the link between the organising function and the organisational structure.

5. Write brief notes on:
   a. delegation, centralisation and decentralisation
   b. span of control
   c. resistance to control in organisations.
6. Describe the management function of control. Illustrate your answer with examples applicable to the construction process.
7. Discuss the benefits for an architectural practice of using a break-even chart.
8. Discuss two commonly used methods of control in organisations, and apply these methods to an organisation in the built environment.

6

COMMUNICATION

Learning outcomes

Following study of this chapter you will be able to:
- define communication and recognise its importance for every manager
- recognise the characteristics of useful information
- understand the communication process
- identify the barriers to effective communication
- explain how to overcome barriers to effective communication.

6.1 Communication defined

Organisational communication can be defined as (ACAS 1982):

> the provision and passing of information and instructions which enable a company or any employing organisation to function efficiently and employees to be properly informed about developments. It covers information of all kinds which can be provided; the channels along which it passes; and the means of passing it.

Griffin (2008) defined communication as *the process of transmitting information from one person to another*. From these two definitions, it is evident that communication is a process of creating, transmitting and interpreting information between two or more people.

Effective communication, then, is the process of sending a message so that the message received is as close as possible in meaning to the message intended. Effective communication is based on the ideas of meaning and consistency of meaning. *Meaning* is the idea which the individual who initiates the communication exchange wishes to convey. With effective communication the meaning is transmitted in such a way that the receiving person properly understands the exchange.

Construction projects can be complex in terms of design, construction and the contractual relationships with clients. The role of communication in this process is very important. Clients are generally advised to develop a project brief which states their needs and which can subsequently be used to test the design solutions offered by the design team. As design teams tend to use a great deal of technical data (e.g.

engineering studies) and graphical media (drawings and models) it is important to ensure that the communication system will enable the client to receive and send information in an effective and timely manner.

6.2 The purposes of communication in organisations

Communication among individuals and groups is vital in all organisations. The primary purpose of communication is **to achieve co-ordinated action**. Without communication, an organisation would be merely a collection of individual employees doing separate tasks. Organisational action would lack co-ordination and be oriented toward individual rather than organisational goals. In the built environment, all parties need to have a clear understanding of what is expected of them. On a construction project, most of the required information is available in the form of drawings, programmes (such as the master programme developed by the main contractor) and specifications. It is very important that the information is understandable in order that it can be interpreted correctly and used to achieve the project goals.

A second purpose of communication is **information sharing**, for example information relating to organisational goals, which give employees a sense of purpose and direction. Another information-sharing function of communication is to give specific task directions to individuals. Information on organisational goals gives employees a sense of how their activities fit into the overall picture; task communication tells them what their job duties are and are not. Employees should also receive information on the results of their efforts, as in performance appraisals. A manager, for example, describes a company policy to an engineer, a brick/blocklayer explains to an apprentice how to achieve the correct ratio of concrete; and a senior quantity surveyor explains to a junior quantity surveyor how to prepare a bill of quantities.

Communication is also essential to the **decision-making process**, as discussed in Chapter 3. Information, and thus information sharing, is needed to define problems, generate and evaluate alternatives, implement decisions, and control and evaluate results.

Communication also relates directly to the basic management functions of **planning**, **organising**, **leading** and **controlling**. Delegation, co-ordination, and organisational change and development also entail communication. Developing reward systems and interacting with subordinates as part of the leading function would be impossible without some form of communication. Communication is also essential to establishing standards, monitoring performance and taking corrective actions as part of control. In the built environment, as in most environments, communication occurs both externally and internally with a number of companies.

A building client who wishes to make a change to the design of a project during the construction stage needs to be careful in communicating the required change to ensure that the project is not adversely affected. It might seem logical to the client to direct the contractor to make the change he or she requires, for example using a different layout for a group of offices. This communication approach, however, will invariably lead to difficulties. First, the client does not have the power under the building contract to direct the contractor—this power rests with the architect. An architect should only direct changes when he or she has established that the changes are of benefit to the project and will not result in unacceptable consequences such as an overall delay to the project, a cost over-run or a reduction in quality. In this instance the correct communication route for the client is to discuss the change with his or her architect and design team.

Finally, communication **expresses feelings and emotions**. People in organisations, like people anywhere else, need to communicate emotions such as happiness, anger, displeasure, confidence and fear. Clearly, then, communication is a pervasive part of virtually all managerial activities.

6.3 Characteristics of useful information

According to Mintzberg (1973), managers spend over half of their daily work schedule communicating; a typical day would include attending scheduled and unscheduled meetings, making and receiving telephone calls, and writing, reading and answering correspondence. As communication is a large part of a manager's daily work life, it is important that the information that is being communicated is useful.

Useful communication generally has four attributes. It should be:
- *Accurate*—the information being transmitted must provide a manager with real and valid facts; for example, a balance sheet should illustrate the accurate financial position of an organisation. In the built environment, a lot of information will come from drawings, programmes and specifications, but the manager must be able to communicate these clearly and accurately in order for all of the information to be understood.
- *Timely*—the information has to be available in time for managers to choose an appropriate course of action; for example, if a manager is sitting on an interview board, he or she needs to have, in advance, copies of the relevant details of candidates selected for interview. In the built environment, if a delivery for concrete has been delayed, but this has not been communicated to the site manager, resources will be wasted: for example, labourers will be waiting for the delivery to arrive.
- *Complete*—the information should enable a manager to understand the full context of a situation. Where information is incomplete, a manager may hold an inaccurate account of an organisation or context. A financial controller, for example, will require information on the financial situation of all departments in order to assess the overall financial state of a particular organisation.

A quantity surveyor preparing a bill of quantities at tender stage will need information, such as drawings and specifications, to be complete and accurate. This is particularly relevant for new forms of government contract because, once the contract price has been agreed, variations during the project will not be accommodated, which means that all details must be in order and complete before a project goes to tender.

- *Relevant*—if the information is to be useful, it must be relevant to the circumstances of the particular managers involved; for example, production managers require details of levels of production achieved, whereas marketing managers require details of advertising rates and sales. The information relevant to the various people involved in a construction project may be similar but will be utilised for different purposes. Some information required by contract managers, planners and estimators will be similar but they will each require the information for different reasons and in a different format.

6.4 Types of communication in organisations

Organisational communication consists of **informal communication**, which includes 'grapevine' rumours, gossip and general conversation, and **formal communication**, whether written, oral, or graphic.

To decide which method of communication is most effective for information, managers generally need to ask themselves:

- *What* needs to be communicated?
- *When* should something be communicated?
- *How* should something be communicated?
- *Where* should communication be held?
- *Who* should be communicated with?

Oral communication

Oral communication consists of face-to-face conversation, telephone calls, formal presentations, departmental meetings, teleconferencing and group discussions. Oral communication is the most prevalent form of organisational communication. Oral communication is particularly powerful because it includes not only speakers' words but also their changes in tone, pitch, speed and volume. As listeners, people use all these cues to understand oral messages.

The primary advantage of oral communication is that it promotes prompt feedback and interchange in the form of spoken questions or agreement, facial expressions, and gestures. Oral communication is typically easy (as all the sender needs to do is talk), and it can be done with little preparation. Oral communication, however, has drawbacks. It may suffer from problems of inaccuracy if the speaker chooses the wrong words to convey meaning or leaves out pertinent details, if noise disrupts the process, or if the receiver forgets part or all of the message. A two-way discussion seldom allows time for a thoughtful, considered response, or for introducing many new facts, and there is no permanent record of what has been said. It allows for immediate feedback and re-explanation, but it may suffer from misinterpretation and inaccuracy if the speaker chooses inappropriate words to convey information. The popular voicemail has all the characteristics of traditional oral communication except there is no feedback. The sender just leaves the message on the machine with no feedback or confirmation that the message was, or will be, received. With no confirmation, the sender does not know for sure that the message will be received as the sender intended it.

Meetings are widely used in the built environment to exchange information, create ideas, discuss problems and agree on decisions. There are generally two types of meeting in relation to a construction project: project meetings and site meetings. The following table highlights the use of each.

Table 6.1 The use of project meetings and site meetings in the built environment (Fryer 1997)

Project Meetings	Site Meetings
Ensure that all parties involved in the project understand the project requirements and are clear about the contractual, design and production details.	Ensure that control is being kept over contractual responsibilities and projected targets in terms of progress, safety, quality and cost.
Proper records are kept, ensuring that contractual responsibilities are being met.	Make sure that the work of both the main contractor and sub-contractors are being effectively co-ordinated.
Monitor the progress of the work, and compare with projected targets.	Highlight any problems such as delays and agree on action to deal with them.
Discuss issues that may affect the budget and time frame of the projects.	Ensure that all documentation from tender through contract to construction is in order.
Ensure that both contractors and sub-contractors are meeting their obligations.	Identify any issues which may cause problems with trade unions such as working conditions and safety.

Written communication

This comprises memos, letters, notes, e-mails, company newspapers, noticeboards, company reports and internal and external post, the Internet and corporate intranets. Following up with a written summary can solve many of the problems of oral communication. Written communication should be accurate and provide a record of the information exchanged. The information can be drafted and revised by the sender before it is transmitted, and the receiver can take time to reread it if necessary. Written communication, however, is slower with regard to feedback and the exchange of ideas.

Many forms of written communication in the built environment are regulated by procedures with organisational or professional codes of conduct, Companies, for example, will have certain templates to deal with various reports. A tender report issued by a quantity surveying company will have the same layout and structure as all of the company's projects. Similarly, certificates of recommendations for payment, issued by the quantity surveyor to the architect and the main contractor, will have a set structure to reflect the payment system for the project, highlighting issues such as the rate of retention being held on payments to the main contractor.

The biggest single drawback of written communication is that it inhibits immediate feedback and interchange. If there is a misunderstanding, it will take longer to recognise and rectify it.

Non-verbal communication

Non-verbal communication is any communication that does not use words. It relies on facial expression, gestures, body movements and physical contact, and is a powerful form of communication. A study by Eisenhardt *et al.* (1997) found that words accounted for only seven per cent of the content of the message, whereas 55 per cent of the content was transmitted by facial expression and body language and another 38 per cent was transmitted by tone.

Electronic communication

This has taken on much greater importance in organisations in recent years. Both formal information systems and personal information technology have reshaped how people communicate with one another. E-mail systems, the Internet, corporate intranets and teleconferences all help to clarify and speed communication in organisations. Electronic communication helps companies in the built environment who have offices spread over a town or city, or in different countries, to communicate effectively.

Choosing a form of communication

The choice of a form of communication depends on a particular situation. For example, oral communication is suited to personal, short communications and non-routine situations; written communication is suited to impersonal, longer communications and routine situations. Managers often combine oral and written communication. All the above types of communicate operate both externally and internally within an organisation. In relation to a construction company, the following internal and external communications take place:
* Internal—within company environments, to other departments, offices and project sites where construction work is taking place.
* External—relates directly to the parties during the various stages of the development of the project.

The extent and type of communication will depend on the project and the type of contract being used.

6.5 The flow of communication in organisations

Communication is frequently classified by its route in companies and project organisations—downward, upward and horizontal being the most common classifications.

Downward communication (top down) occurs when information comes down the hierarchy from managers to employees. Examples of downward communication are:

- company newspapers
- employee reports
- general information that higher-level managers think will be of value to lower-level managers and employees.

Upward communication occurs when messages are sent from employees to managers. Examples of upward communication are:

- suggestion schemes
- questionnaires
- surveys

Upward communication is usually passed through an immediate supervisor, to a lower-level manager, and then to higher-level managers.

Horizontal communication occurs between individuals and teams or between departments and work groups and involves colleagues and peers at the same level in an organisation. Organisations with flatter structures tend to make greater use of horizontal communication between employees who work on similar tasks or specialised situations. Some horizontal communication occurs between people of generally the same status (for example a consultant to the contracts manager), whereas some horizontal communication occurs between people with functional relationships (for example between a plant manager and site supervisor).

Horizontal communication serves a number of purposes.

- It facilitates co-ordination among interdependent departments.
- It can be used for joint problem-solving.
- It plays a major role in work teams whose members are drawn from several departments.

On a construction project, communication between the main contractor and the sub-contractors may give rise to downward communication and horizontal communication. The sub-contractors' representative on site will have loyalties to their own company, with whom they will communicate laterally. The same person will communicate vertically with the main contractor on site and will have to ensure that loyalties to their own company do not affect the lines of communication with the main contractor.

6.6 Steps in developing effective communication

Managers need to understand the steps involved in the communication process in order to ensure that their communication process is effective. There are nine elements in the communication process, with the *sender* and *receiver* being the key elements (see Figure 6.1).

1. *Sender*—a person (the sender) transmitting a message to someone, for example a manager notifying employees regarding a training course.
2. *Encoding*—the process of conveying the intended message through, for example, words, illustrations and body language. Effective encoding is an ongoing issue in the built environment: drawings are often issued incomplete or out of date.
3. *Message*—the actual information which, for example, might contain the time, date, location and content of a seminar and details of the presenters.
4. *Media*—the communication channels through which a message moves from sender to receiver, for example, e-mails, letters, drawings, faxes, telephone calls, memos. In the built environment these methods are heavily relied upon because they are cheap and communicate the information quickly.
5. *Decoding*—interpretations of a message by those receiving the message; the content and the perceived relevance of the communication influence the decoding.
6. *Receiver*—the person receiving the message.
7. *Response*—the reactions of the receiver; for example, employees may react positively, neutrally, sceptically or negatively.
8. *Feedback*—the receiver's response communicated to the sender.
9. *Noise*—unplanned distortion during the process which may disrupt communication, for example mistaken recollections of an original message may be passed on as a result of distortion.

Figure 6.1 The communication process

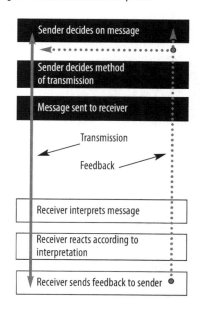

6.7 Barriers to effective communication

Communication skills are important for all managers. There are, however, numerous factors that can hinder communication or act as barriers to effective communication, the most common of these being:

- *Predispositions and individual bias*—receivers of communications may already have their minds firmly set in a certain way or may have a bias influenced by cultural background or personal values.
- *Reluctance to communicate*—employees may be reluctant to communicate with their manager because of fear, or because they believe their manager does not value their opinions.
- *Information overload*—employees may be receiving more information than they can effectively handle. In the built environment, companies will be dealing with several projects at the same time, so a considerable amount of information will be communicated at any one time.
- *Status differences*—higher-level managers, for example, may not be interested in hearing what new employees have to say.
- *Cultural differences*—will influence the way in which a worker responds to new rulings. Some cultures may have less stringent rules about, for example, wearing health and safety equipment.
- *Poor listening skills*—individuals may not have developed their listening skills, resulting in, for example, delegates at a meeting not paying attention and failing to recall what has been said.
- *Noise*—any unintended interference with effective communication; noise may include sounds, or other distractions not associated with sound, that are not relevant to a communication, such as visual distractions, talk from other employees, emotional upsets or physical discomfort. Construction sites are noisy and therefore can present many distractions which can affect face-to-face communication.
- *Verbal difficulties*—can include the use of jargon or technical words which the receiver may not understand, for example formwork, water–cement ratio, planning supervisor.
- *Distance*—designers tend to be separated from contractors, and a construction site may be a long distance from the company's headquarters. This puts a limit on face-to-face communication and non-verbal communication.

Overcoming the barriers to successful communication

The following methods help to overcome some of these barriers to communication.
- *Predispositions and individual bias*—individuals should be encouraged to approach communication with an open mind and be willing to change their views; people are often unaware of their own biases until they are brought to their attention.
- *Reluctance to communicate*—a 'blame-free' organisational culture will encourage employees to communicate freely and will demonstrate that employees' opinions are valued.
- *Information overload*—the amount of communication transmitted to employees should be limited and communication should always be relevant and appropriate to employee needs.

- *Status differences*—upward communication should be valued and employees should be actively encouraged to communicate across all levels of an organisation.
- *Poor listening skills*—proactive listening skills should be learned; essentially, this means not interrupting the speaker; concentrating on the speaker's words and their meaning; listening with patience; and showing interest.
- *Noise*—improvements in the working environment and attempts to eliminate distractions may be required.
- *Verbal difficulties*—the language used should be clear and easy to understand and jargon and over-technical language should be avoided.

6.8 Key points

Communication is the process of transmitting information from one person to another. *Effective communication* is the process of a sender transmitting a message to a receiver in such a way that the message received is as close as possible in meaning to the message intended.

Various forms of communication are used in organisations. These include oral, written, and non-verbal communication. Organisational communication may be formal or informal. *Vertical communication* between managers and employees may be both upward and downward. *Horizontal communication* involves colleagues at the same level communicating with each other.

If the information to be communicated is to be useful, it must be accurate, timely, complete and relevant. In order for communication to be effective it is important that the sender clearly encodes the message and transmits it accurately to one or more receivers, who receive the message and decode it into meaning.

There are a number of *barriers* that hinder the communication process. Managers need to recognise these barriers and understand how to overcome them. Generally barriers can be identified at both the individual and organisational level. Similarly, individual and organisational solutions may be used to overcome these barriers.

Important terms and concepts

barriers to communication (p. 108)
certificate of recommendation for payment (p. 105)
characteristics of useful information (p. 103)
co-ordinated action (p. 102)
decision-making (p. 102)
decoding (p. 108)
downward communication (p. 107)
effective communication (p. 108)
electronic communication (p. 106)

Questions for review

1. Evaluate the importance of effective communication in an organisation in the built environment which is undergoing rapid *organisational* change.
2. Evaluate the importance of effective communication in a rapidly changing organisation in the built environment which is undergoing *technological* change.
3. Describe barriers to effective communication in an organisation in the built environment. Suggest how these barriers might be overcome.
4. Explain how a manager can combine oral, written and non-verbal communication into an effective communication system *at site level* during a construction project.
5. Explain how a manager can combine oral, written and non-verbal communication into an effective communication system *within a design team* during the design stage of a construction project.
6. Discuss the advantages of effective communications in the built environment.
7. What are the components of the communication process for an organisation operating in the built environment?

7

MOTIVATION

Learning outcomes

Following study of this chapter you will be able to:
*   explain what motivation is
*   describe the major *content* perspectives on motivation
*   describe the major *process* perspectives on motivation
*   highlight the motivating characteristics common to a number of motivational theories.

7.1 Motivation defined

Motivation has been defined by Steers and Porter (1991) as *the set of forces that cause people to behave in certain ways.*

Motivation theorists aim to discover the motive, or drive, that triggers and sustains particular behaviours of individuals. Motivation refers to both the *internal* and *external* forces that direct people's behaviour.

The study of motivation is important for managers because motivated staff work well. Work motivation is a psychological concept that is primarily concerned with increasing the direction of employees' work-related behaviours to positively influence performance output. The ability of managers to make the workforce productive is vital to the success of projects. Motivation aims to successfully balance interconnected motivation factors that help increase worker satisfaction. The built environment is an industry with distinctive characteristics which affect the motivation of employees. Each construction project is unique, as it comprises non-routine events subject to changing weather, variable ground conditions, industrial relations and historical practices which are quite different from those in mainstream manufacturing industries. While there are many theories of motivation, there is no simple answer to the question, 'How do you motivate employees?'

7.2 Historical perspectives on motivation

The traditional approach

The **traditional approach** to motivation is best represented by the work of Frederick W. Taylor. As noted in Chapter 1, Taylor advocated an incentive pay system. He believed that managers know more than workers about the jobs being performed, and he assumed that money is the primary motivator for everyone. Other assumptions of the traditional approach were that work is unpleasant for most people and that the money they earn is more important than the nature of the job they are performing. Hence, people could be expected to perform any kind of job if they are paid enough. Although the role of money as a motivating factor cannot be dismissed today, the traditional approach took a very narrow view of the role of monetary compensation and also failed to consider other motivational factors. Hague (1985) argued that bonus, payment by results and financial incentives have given rise to increasing industrial relations problems in the built environment. However, many of the motivational methods used by managers in the built environment have developed from the traditional approach.

The human relations approach

This approach emphasised the role of social processes in the workplace (see Chapter 1). Human relations theorists emphasised that employees want to feel useful and important, that employees have strong social needs (e.g. friends at work), and that these needs are more important than money in motivating employees. Proponents of the human relations approach advised managers to motivate employees by allowing them self-direction and self-control in carrying out activities.

The human resource approach

The human resource approach to motivation assumes that employees are motivated by their contribution and participation and that these are valuable to both individuals and organisations. **Participation** is the process of giving employees a voice in making decisions about their work. The human resource approach assumes that employees want to contribute and are able to make genuine contributions. The task of managers, therefore, is to encourage participation and to create a work environment which makes full use of the human resources available. This approach guides most contemporary thinking about employee motivation.

Closely linked with participation is empowerment. **Empowerment** is the process of enabling workers to set their own work goals, make decisions, and solve problems within their sphere of responsibility and authority. Empowerment promotes participation in many areas including the work itself, the work context and the work environment. Empowerment often occurs naturally on a construction project; for example, the project team is made up of skilled workers from different backgrounds, who all need to be self-motivated and work on their own initiative to achieve the project goals.

7.3 Motivation theories

Motivation theories analyse employee performance and how work and its rewards satisfy individual employee needs. Employees have basic needs or expectations which, if not satisfied, stimulate behaviour directed towards satisfying those needs. One basic model of motivation suggests the presence of a stimulus (a physical drive or need), followed by a behaviour of some kind which leads to a satisfactory or unsatisfactory response or outcome (Figure 7.1).

Figure 7.1 Basic model of motivation

Motivational theories are generally divided into content and process theories. **Content theories** concentrate on what motivates people, for example, the factors that motivate people. **Process theories** concentrate on why people choose to behave in certain ways and how motivation is aroused and maintained.

7.4 Content theories of motivation

Maslow's hierarchy of needs

During the 1940s, Abraham Maslow, an American organisational psychologist, was one of the first to classify human needs or motives. Maslow suggested that human needs may be classified into motivating factors that influence behaviour. He proposed that these needs are based on a hierarchical model, with basic needs at the bottom and higher needs at the top (see Figure 7.2).

According to Maslow's hierarchy, most people are motivated by the desire to satisfy a group of five specific needs. Starting from the bottom of the hierarchy, these needs are:

- *Physiological needs*—for example, food, sleep, and air, which represent basic requirements of survival; in an organisational setting, examples of these needs include:
  - comfortable temperatures
  - adequate lighting
  - an environment generally conducive to work.
- *Safety and security needs*—a company in the built environment should aim to maintain a high level of job security and safety in the public domain in order to meet employees' basic needs in the work environment, to motivate existing employees and to attract new employees to the company. Providing regular training for employees in health and safety should reduce the threat of any

accidents occurring. Some examples of safety and security needs are:
- a salary
- a safe working environment (safety training is compulsory for most employees in the built environment)
- job continuity
- a pension plan
- a grievance system.
- *Belongingness needs*—induction programmes for new employees to introduce them to the company objectives, existing employees, the facilities and the working environment can help satisfy belongingness needs. Examples of these needs include:
  - friends at work
  - teamwork
  - social interaction at work.
- *Esteem needs*—for example, the need for a positive self-image, self-esteem, status, and the need for recognition and respect from others; in an organisational setting, examples of these needs are:
  - a sense of accomplishment
  - a job title.
- *Self-actualisation needs*—for example, the need for self-fulfilment, achievement and continued individual development; in an organisational setting, these needs can be met by:
  - a challenging job
  - participation in making decisions about one's work
  - opportunities for further learning
  - activities that contribute to a sense of fulfilment.

Figure 7.2 Maslow's hierarchy of needs

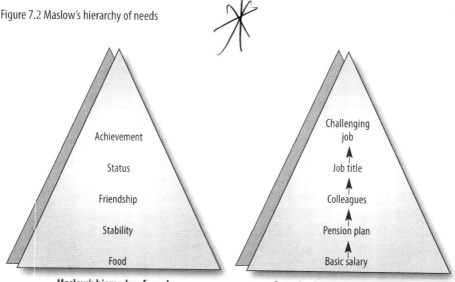

Maslow's hierarchy of needs

Achievement

Status

Friendship

Stability

Food

Maslow's hierarchy of needs

Challenging job

Job title

Colleagues

Pension plan

Basic salary

Organisational hierarchy of needs

Maslow believed that people tend to satisfy their needs systematically, beginning with the basic physiological needs and then moving up the hierarchy. Maslow further suggested that as long as physiological needs remain unsatisfied, an individual is motivated to fulfil them alone. When physiological needs have been satisfied, an individual then moves 'up' the hierarchy and is concerned with safety and security needs. The individual continues to move 'up' until self-actualisation-level needs are reached.

A frequent criticism of Maslow's theory is that, at any given time, different people are likely to be striving to fulfil different need levels of the hierarchy. The model assumes that one motive or drive should predominate at any moment in time, whereas individuals may actually be working simultaneously for pay (security), social interaction (belongingness) and status (self-esteem). Some individuals may also choose to satisfy their needs outside their workplace, for example through sport or other leisure activities. Maslow's theory, however, has illustrated that people have a variety of needs, the satisfaction of which may be pursued at work, and that managers need to understand these needs in order to motivate employees. Maslow's theory can be applied to the built environment by viewing a construction company in totality (Table 7.1).

Table 7.1 Applying Maslow's hierarchy of needs to employees in the construction industry

Need	Application to Employees in the Construction Industry
Physiological	Employees who are based on site throughout the duration of a construction project will require adequate site offices, with suitable facilities that ensure comfortable and favourable working conditions.
Safety and security	Safe Pass training must be provided to all new employees in a construction company to satisfy their safety needs. Another need that employees will seek is job security; however, this is difficult for many construction companies to guarantee in the current economic climate.
Belongingness	Social interaction is an important need for construction employees. As different work groups will be working on different projects it is important for companies to ensure that all employees are being included. Employees, for example, must be informed in time of a site or project meeting. Employees should be informed of any corporate events taking place and given the opportunity to attend.
Esteem	When an employee has successfully completed their tasks as part of a complex or unusual project, managers acknowledging a 'job well done' will improve en employee's job satisfaction and self-esteem.
Self-actualisation	An architect who has designed a building which has been nominated for, or awarded, an Irish Architecture Award from the RIAI contributes to a sense of fulfilment.

Alderfer's ERG model

A variation of Maslow's model was proposed by Alderfer in 1969, arguing that individual needs were best explained on a continuum, rather than in a hierarchy. Alderfer believed that there are only three major sets of needs:

- *Existence needs* (E)—for example, the basic requirements of life; that is, a combination of Maslow's physiological and safety needs. In relation to employees in the built environment, this may be interpreted as the need for a competitive salary in addition to safety on site to protect workers from physical harm.
- *Relatedness needs* (R)—for example, social and interpersonal needs, reflecting Maslow's social or belongingness needs level. In relation to an employee in the construction industry, this could be identified in a preference for working as a member of a group (e.g. a gang of carpenters) rather than alone, which may result in the worker feeling isolated from colleagues.
- *Growth needs* (G)—for example, personal development needs; this is a combination of Maslow's self-esteem and self-actualisation needs. In the construction industry, for example, a progression path may exist whereby a carpenter on site can develop his or her skills and attend supervisory training to achieve promotion to the position of trade foreperson.

Alderfer's research findings, based on 110 questionnaires distributed to bank officials of various levels, suggested that the less a higher-order need was satisfied the more likely it was that an individual would revert to satisfying the next level of need below, even though it had previously been satisfied. Alderfer concluded, therefore, that needs are not determined hierarchically. The following table illustrates Alderfer's model applied to a construction worker.

Table 7.2 Applying Alderfer's model to a construction worker

Need	Application to a Construction Worker on a Construction Site
Existence	A joiner on site will need certain tools to commence work and clear instruction from his or her supervisor in relation to what needs to be done and the reward (financial) for achieving the task. The joiner will also need to know that his or her job will be safe for the duration of the project so that he or she can commit fully to the work.
Relatedness	Typically, the joiner will want to feel part of a team and enjoy the camaraderie of work colleagues. Often the group will share knowledge and may have a sharing mechanism for the disbursement of financial rewards related to the work tasks.
Growth	The joiner, like most craftspeople, will take pride in the completion of his/her work and will actively seek to express his/her craft and mastery by completing challenging work. This will afford the joiner the opportunity to develop and grow within their craft.

McClelland's achievement motivation

Research conducted by David McClelland (1961) of Harvard University stressed the importance of individual differences in motivation. McClelland and his team conducted research with over five hundred managers from twenty-five different organisations in the United States to determine what motivates a good manager. Their research findings suggest that managers possess three basic motivational needs:

- need for achievement (n-Ach)
- need for power (n-Pow)
- need for affiliation (n-Aff).

McClelland believed that managers who have a high need for achievement (n-Ach) are influenced by childhood experiences that gave them independence at an early age and by cultural backgrounds that expected competence from them. He concluded that, if the need for achievement is strongly influenced by environmental factors, employees can be motivated to achieve through training programmes. McClelland also stated that managers with a high need for achievement will be attracted to entrepreneurial rather than bureaucratic organisations.

McClelland found that managers who did not score high on the need for achievement may score high on the need for affiliation (n-Aff), meaning that these managers will be concerned with having approval from both their employees and superiors and will be sensitive to the needs of others. He also suggested that managers who are concerned with the needs of others are still interested in getting the job done, which in turn should lead to greater organisational effectiveness.

McClelland's research also illustrated that good interpersonal skills are important for managers, particularly when combined with a need to influence people for the overall good of an organisation. Managers who forcefully express their opinions and who like being in control of events have a greater need for power (n-Pow) than to achieve or to be liked. The concept of power in organisations is closely linked to leadership; for example, McClelland suggested that higher-level managers in organisations tended to be associated with a low level of affiliation and a moderate-to-high need for power.

Overall, McClelland's research is important as it recognises that people do not share similar needs to the same extent. His research findings also proposed that some important needs are not inherited but learned. In comparison with other content theories of motivation, McClelland's work looks more towards the development of senior managers. Many managers in the built environment are likely to be self-motivated and possess the three motivational needs outlined by McClelland. Table 7.3 illustrates examples of the application of McClelland's motivation needs to construction professionals.

Table 7.3 Applying McClelland's motivational needs to construction professionals

McClelland's Motivational Need	Application to Construction Professionals
Need for Achievement	Construction professionals, such as architects, engineers and quantity surveyors, will normally possess a strong desire for achievement, both personally as a professional and collectively as a team working on behalf of a client. The need for achievement is strong for these professionals, as completing a difficult project successfully and keeping a good working relationship with a client can lead to repeat business and overall job satisfaction.
Need for Power	Within most design teams, individuals will seek opportunities to gain power, to enable them to promote their own ideas, which in turn will satisfy their motivational needs. If the need for power is maintained at a healthy level, it can be positive for the overall project in the competitive environment. The need for individual power, however, must not be allowed to interfere with the overall project or to undermine individuals, not all of whom may have a need for power.
Need for Affiliation	For a design team to function at a high level, each individual member must believe that their contribution is accommodated and appreciated in a positive manner by the other members of the group. This fosters a culture of affiliation and will strengthen the working norms of the design team.

Herzberg's two-factor theory

Frederick Herzberg (1959) developed his two-factor theory of motivation by concentrating on satisfaction at work. Herzberg and his team interviewed two hundred accountants and engineers and asked them to recall when they had experienced satisfactory and unsatisfactory feelings about their jobs.

The research concluded that two different factors affect motivation at work. The factors influencing satisfaction are called *motivation factors* and are specifically related to the content of the work involved. The factors which remove dissatisfaction are called *hygiene factors* and are related to the adequacy of work conditions. The research suggested that, while hygiene factors help to remove dissatisfaction, they do not necessarily provide satisfaction as the absence of dissatisfaction does not equate to satisfaction. Motivation factors, on the other hand, push individuals to achieve greater performance.

Herzberg suggested that hygiene factors and dissatisfiers (the lack of hygiene factors) relate more to the environment than to work content. The major difference between hygiene and motivators is that adequate hygiene factors can prevent dissatisfaction, whereas motivators can bring positive satisfaction. Employees generally assume that hygiene factors should be in place, and may take them for granted, but if they are not in place, employees tend to be dissatisfied. For example, a construction site can be a difficult environment for workers. The provision of good on-site facilities to cater for their welfare (canteen facilities, wet weather drying-out facilities, on-site medical hut, clean and accessible toilet facilities, car parking, secure tool storage, etc.) would all be considered hygiene factors. If these hygiene factors are not present dissatisfaction can result. Attempts to improve motivation are unlikely to be successful until these hygiene factors have been improved. Examples of motivation and hygiene factors common on construction sites in the built environment are shown in Table 7.4.

Table 7.4 Motivation and hygiene factors on construction sites

Hygiene Factors Leading to Employee Satisfaction	Motivation Factors Leading to Employee Satisfaction
Canteen facilities	Challenging work
Medical facilities on site	Responsibility
Provision of drying-out facilities during inclement weather	Recognition
Secure storage facilities for workers' tools	Clearly defined goals
Toilet and washroom facilities	Achievement
Pay and security	
Interpersonal relationships	

A criticism of Herzberg's theory is that his sample of accountants and engineers was not representative of the general population, and his theories need further research to prove their validity generally. The theory, however, has led to designing jobs that contain a greater number of motivators.

McGregor's Theory X and Theory Y

McGregor's Theory X and Theory Y (1960) are classifications of two sets of assumptions about behaviour. McGregor believed that managers classified employee behaviour as either Theory X or Theory Y, as illustrated in Table 7.5.

Table 7.5 McGregor's Theory X and Theory Y

Theory X	Theory Y
Employees are lazy and dislike work.	Employees like work.
Employees need to be controlled and coerced.	Employees do not have to be controlled or coerced.
Employees dislike responsibility.	Employees accept and seek responsibility.
Employees want only security and material rewards.	Employees want intrinsic rewards and are creative and imaginative.

McGregor argued that Theory X represented the views of scientific management theorists and Theory Y represented the human relations approach. A Theory X approach assumes that employees dislike work and need to be tightly controlled.

The only way to improve their productivity is to simplify the production process and supervise the employees closely. He suggested that, under the right conditions, Theory Y managers could motivate staff to exercise self-direction and control and to apply their intellect to problems as they arise. Theory X and Theory Y identify two extreme forms of management style. A mixture of the two styles, however, is likely to produce a more effective managerial approach.

7.5 Process theories of motivation

Equity theory

When employees are motivated to behave in certain ways, they assess the fairness or equity of their behaviour. Equity theory matches the notion of 'an honest day's work for an honest day's pay'. Equity is an employee's belief that the treatment or reward he or she receives is equitable to the treatment that other employees receive. Employees assess their inputs, such as education, experience and effort, in relation to the outcomes they receive, including pay, promotional prospects, benefits and recognition, working conditions, etc. Equity theory proposes that employees view their inputs and outcomes as a ratio and then compare their ratio to that of another employee or other employees with similar circumstances:

$$\frac{\text{Outcomes (self)}}{\text{Inputs (self)}} = \frac{\text{Outcomes (other)}}{\text{Inputs (other)}}$$

The comparisons and ratios are very subjective and are based on individual perceptions. After comparisons have been made, an individual may feel under-rewarded, equitably rewarded or over-rewarded. A feeling of equity will occur when the two ratios are equal. Equity theory suggests that employees are not only interested in rewards but also interested in *comparative* rewards. Such rewards, however, are best applied to *extrinsic* rewards, such as pay, promotion and benefits, rather than *intrinsic* rewards, such as personal achievement and responsibility, as the latter are personal to the individual and less capable of objective comparison.

In the built environment, the feeling of inequity can cause conflicts between directly employed labour and sub-contracted labour where one group is working under a more favourable set of working conditions than the other. On heavy engineering projects it is often necessary to import specialist labour, for example welders from the UK; and occasionally, these welders were paid in sterling, particularly in times when sterling was strong against the local currency (the punt and later the euro). Clearly, paying such a differential to workers carrying out identical work led to Irish workers expressing their grievances about the inequity of the situation. Local arrangements have been used to resolve the situation, which has resulted in an agreement under which Irish welders have been paid in sterling on an equal basis to their UK counterparts.

Expectancy theory

Expectancy theory is based on the work of Victor Vroom in the 1960s and focuses on how employees perceive the relationships between:
- effort
- performance
- rewards.

Expectancy theory suggests that employees will be motivated to act only when they have a reasonable expectancy that their behaviour will lead to the outcomes they desire (Figure 7.3). Motivational strength therefore increases if there are positive expectations of work outcomes, that is, how much an employee wants something and how likely he or she thinks they are to achieve it. On construction sites bonuses are often used to encourage work crews to achieve difficult deadlines. The work crews will evaluate the degree of effort required to achieve the deadline and will determine if the bonus is sufficient to reward the additional expected effort. If the workers believe the expected effort will be properly rewarded, their motivation level is likely to be high.

Figure 7.3 Expectancy theory

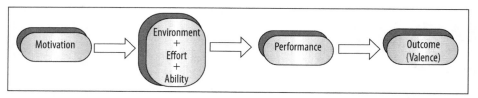

Expectancy theory assumes that:
1. Behaviour is determined by a set of forces, both in the individual and in the work environment.
2. Employees choose to make decisions about their own performance in organisations depending on their own needs, desires and goals.
3. Employees make decisions regarding their behaviour according to their perceptions of the extent to which their behaviour might lead to desired outcomes.

Vroom concluded that performance leads to various outcomes, each of which has an associated value called its valence. **Valence** is the strength of belief in the likelihood of the occurrence of an associated attractive reward.

Vroom also classed rewards as *intrinsic* and *extrinsic*. Employees can exercise a degree of personal control over intrinsic rewards, for example fulfilling higher-level personal needs and self-esteem. Extrinsic rewards, such as pay and other working conditions, are generally outside the control of an employee as these rewards are provided by the organisation. Rewards associated with intrinsic factors are more likely to produce job satisfaction.

Goal-setting theory

Goal-setting theory suggests that motivation is based on goals or objectives that employees set for themselves. Research by Locke (1968) confirmed that employee performance improved when employees set specific rather than vague goals. The research also found that, given adequate levels of ability and commitment by employees, more difficult goals tend to elicit greater performance than easier goals would. Goals, however, must not be so difficult that they are unattainable. Research by Cooper (1995) found that workers on construction sites who were encouraged to take part in the goal-setting process performed better than workers on site where the goal-setting theory was not used. Goal-setting theory also suggests that the rate of acceptance of and commitment to particular goals will determine employee efforts towards their attainment. Organisational support for employee goals together with employee performance should lead to both intrinsic and extrinsic rewards, which in turn should lead to employee satisfaction.

Reinforcement theory

This motivational process addresses why some behaviours are maintained over time and why other behaviours change. When reinforcement theory is applied to motivation it is linked to learning. The reinforcement theory of motivation suggests that a given behaviour is a product of the consequences of earlier behaviour and proposes that behaviour resulting in positive rewards is likely to be repeated, whereas behaviour resulting in punishment is less likely to be repeated.

Positive reinforcement is a method of strengthening behaviour by providing a reward for a desired behaviour. **Punishment** discourages undesired behaviours by using negative outcomes or unpleasant consequences when undesired behaviour occurs. The conditions of contract set out at the beginning of a construction project would occasionally be viewed as negative reinforcement, as failure to comply with the conditions by one party to the contract will result in claims being made against that party. Building contracts frequently use 'carrot and stick' mechanisms to promote performance by the contractor. The 'carrot' mechanism rewards the contractor for performing well; this can take the form of milestone payments whereby the contractor is entitled to get paid for work once it is completed and not on a traditional monthly basis. The faster the contractor works, the more cash flow can be generated. The 'stick' mechanism typically involves the use of liquidated damages clauses whereby the contractor must pay the client a financial compensation if he or she fails to meet a prescribed deadline. The contractor views these clauses as a punishment for non-performance.

Reinforcement theory is more concerned with controlling the behaviour of employees than with what or how behaviour is motivated. It concerns control and power over others; for example, health and safety requirements dictate how construction workers must perform certain tasks to ensure their personal safety and the safety of others. Requirements for safety training and the use of personal protective equipment help reinforce the safe behaviour required of construction workers.

7.6 The psychological contract

The relationship between employees and employers can be described in many ways. Any relationship is formed within a context of rights, expectations and obligations on the part of each party. Relationships are also influenced by the cultural norms of what is and what is not acceptable about the balance of power within the particular organisation. The balance between the employee and the organisation has been summed up in the phrase 'psychological contract'. The psychological contract is subjective, unwritten, and often not discussed or negotiated. A major feature of psychological contracts is the concept of mutuality—that there is a common and agreed understanding of promises and obligations that the respective parties have made to each other about work, pay, commitment, flexibility, security and career advancement.

The employee, for example, offers:
- loyalty
- conformity to requirements
- commitment to the employer's goals and trust in their employer not to abuse their goodwill.

In return, the employer offers:
- security of employment
- promotion prospects
- training and development
- flexibility.

The psychological contract underpins the work relationship by acting in a similar manner to Herzberg's hygiene factors. Good psychological contracts may not always result in superior performance or, indeed, satisfied employees; but poor psychological contracts tend to act as demotivators, which can be reflected in lower levels of employee commitment, higher levels of absenteeism and turnover, and reduced performance.

The psychological contract between employers and employees in the past was a job for life in return for effort and loyalty. The new-style contract is lifelong employability in exchange for effort. The employer is offering development and experience, which are valuable in employees' current and future roles.

Meeting employees' needs and expectations can be difficult in the built environment because of short-term projects and a disjointed industry. In these recessionary times, however, organisations in the built environment are supporting their employees by providing continuous development opportunities, reskilling and up-skilling opportunities to strengthen the psychological contract. Some companies, for example, are offering to finance workers to return to college on a part-time basis to gain a degree; employees can work part-time for the company while they are studying. This also benefits the organisation, because when organisations are bidding for projects, they will have employees with a wide range of both academic and work-based learning qualifications.

7.7 Key points

Motivation is a force that influences the behaviour of people. It is important for managers to have an understanding of what motivates employees, as motivation, together with ability and environmental factors, determines employee performance. The key to effective work performance lies in an understanding of human motivation.

Overall, there are three motivational perspectives:
- content
- process
- reinforcement.

Content perspectives on motivation are concerned with whatever factors result in motivation. Some of the content theories include:
- Maslow's hierarchy of needs
- Alderfer's ERG model
- McClelland's achievement motivation
- Herzberg's two-factor theory
- McGregor's Theory X and Theory Y.

Process perspectives on motivation are concerned with how motivation occurs. Process perspectives include:
- equity theory
- expectancy theory
- goal-setting theory.

The *reinforcement* perspective on motivation is concerned with how motivation is maintained. It suggests that behaviour resulting in rewarding consequences is likely to be repeated, whereas behaviour resulting in negative consequences is less likely to be repeated.

It is important for managers to realise that there is no 'one best way' to motivate employees. Managers must take account of different situations, psychological variables and the behaviour of employees when motivating individuals. Managers are therefore advised to use a combination of approaches that best suit the circumstances.

Important terms and concepts

Alderfer's ERG model (p. 117)
carrot and stick mechanism (p. 123)
conditions of contract (p. 123)
content theories of motivation (p. 114)
empowerment (p. 113)
equity theory (p. 121)
expectancy theory (p. 122)
goal-setting theory (p. 123)
Herzberg's two-factor theory (p. 119)
human relations approach (p. 113)
human resource approach (p. 113)
liquidated damages clause (p. 123)
Maslow's hierarchy of needs (p. 114)
McClelland's achievement motivation (p. 118)
McGregor's Theory X and Theory Y (p. 120)
participation (p. 113)
positive reinforcement (p. 123)
process theories of motivation (p. 121)
psychological contract (p. 124)
punishment (p. 123)
reinforcement theory (p. 123)
traditional approach (p. 112)

Questions for review

1. Discuss Maslow's theory of needs and outline the relevance of this theory for employee motivation in organisations in the built environment.
2. Identify and discuss various ways in which managers in the built environment can attempt to increase the motivation of employees.
3. What are the differences between motivation and hygiene factors in the two-factor theory?
4. Write brief notes on:
   a. equity theory
   b. expectancy theory
   c. goal-setting theory.
   In each case, specify their relevance to the built environment.
5. Summarise the motivation process.
6. Compare and contrast the content, process and reinforcement perspectives on motivation.

7. Discuss the implications for management of any two theories of motivation, specifically citing examples from the built environment.

8

HUMAN RESOURCE MANAGEMENT

Learning outcomes

Following study of this chapter you will be able to:

- understand the background and the development of human resource management in organisations
- define human resource management
- identify human resource management activities performed by managers
- recognise the contribution of human resource management activities to the overall functioning of organisations.

8.1 Background to human resource management (HRM)

During the 1890s, an increasing number of employers in Britain and North America accepted responsibility for the welfare of their employees. In Britain, organisations such as Cadbury and Rowntree appointed 'industrial welfare' workers, who were responsible for ensuring the well-being of women and children in the workforce and for watching over their health and behaviour.

During the nineteenth century, conditions of work for most employees in factories were very poor. Also during this period, the trade union movement was developing as individuals realised the strength they could gain by coming together to negotiate with employers. Due to the lack of skilled labour during the First World War (1914–18), many women were encouraged to become part of the industrial workforce for the first time. This expanded the role of recruitment and selection functions within organisations and resulted in:

- greater concern for workers' welfare
- making the best possible use of employees.

During the 1920s and 1930s, internal organisational practices were influenced by developments in management theory, for example scientific management and the human relations movement (see Chapter 1). In particular, the Hawthorne experiments highlighted the importance both of integrating employees into the organisation and of the 'controlling' personnel function.

During the Second World War (1939–45), there was an increase in demand for materials and labour—particularly in the armed forces, auxiliary forces and the munitions industries—resulting in increased welfare functions, including the provision of training programmes to maximise labour productivity, and the improvement of morale and motivation.

During the Second World War, joint consultation between management and workforce was practised. There was also an increased emphasis on health and safety and the need for specialists to deal with industrial relations. This resulted in the welfare worker (now to be known as personnel manager, as the term 'welfare' was viewed more as a feminine issue among the increasing number of male employees) becoming the spokesperson for management in discussions with trade unions. This could be regarded as the beginning of the industrial relations function as performed by modern-day human resource managers.

During the 1960s and 1970s, there was a growth in the amount of employment legislation that reinforced the importance of personnel officers in areas such as pay negotiations and dealing with trade unions. During the late 1980s, the term 'human resource management' emerged in Britain. Traditionally, a personnel department was often perceived as an administrative support function with a lowly status. More recently, personnel has become very much part of an organisation's human resource management function, and human resource management is conceived to be more than personnel and to have a wider range than the core personnel function. In order for human resource management to be strategic it had to encompass all the human resource areas of the organisation and to be engaged with by all employees. In addition, decentralisation and devolvement of responsibility are also seen as very much part of the human resource management strategy as it facilitates communication, involvement, and commitment of middle management and other employees within the organisation.

Work in the built environment tends to be very labour intensive because of the large number of workers needed for construction work and the high levels of input required by temporary project teams. Effective management of all personnel involved is vital to the successful completion of a construction project and the efficient management of an organisation.

8.2 Human resource management (HRM) defined

Defining human resource management is still a controversial activity. For some researchers, human resource management is a new approach to managing the labour process. For others, human resource management is simply a re-labelling of personnel management and is viewed as 'old wine in new bottles'. Human resource management has been defined (Bratton and Gold 2003) as:

> That part of the management process that specialises in the management of people in work organisations.

From this definition, individuals in organisations are 'human resources', implying that the management of people is comparable to the management of other organisational resources. More than other resources, however, it is the individuals or the people who make the major difference to an organisation. The human resources also differ from other resources in organisations because individuals have the ability to question and evaluate the actions of management. Employees may also form groups and trade unions to strengthen their positions in organisations.

HRM emphasises that employees are critical to achieving sustainable competitive advantage, that human resource practices need to be integrated with the corporate strategy, and that human resource specialists help organisational controllers to meet both efficiency and equity objectives.

There has been considerable debate and discussion in management literature comparing HRM with traditional personnel management. Researchers agree that while similarities exist between personnel management and HRM, there are some key characteristics which differentiate traditional personnel management from HRM:

- HRM is integrated into strategic planning, as organisations realise that competitive advantage can be achieved through managing people as efficiently and effectively as other resources. This is important in the built environment as the industry can go through boom and recession phases. Maintaining employee levels can help companies sustain a competitive advantage; however, this can be difficult during of a recession.
- HRM emphasises the importance of leadership in creating 'vision', innovation and employee commitment at all levels of the organisation. In the built environment, vision and innovation are important when a construction organisation is at its initial stages or going through growth phases. Innovation can be seen, for example, when an architect designs a unique, one-off building for a client and is committed to transforming his or her vision into reality.
- With HRM, the role of line managers (supervisors) is increased; for example, tasks traditionally undertaken by personnel management are often devolved to line management. In the built environment many site managers are already familiar with their responsibilities in relation to employment issues as they deal with conflicts and human resources-related issues on a daily basis on site when co-ordinating direct employees and sub-contracted workers.
- HRM policies, such as recruitment, selection, rewards and employee relations are fully integrated and consistent with an organisation's culture.

Allowing for the problems of definitions and demarcation lines between various conceptions of human resource management, HRM has become a fashionable concept and a controversial subject since the 1980s, with its boundaries very much overlapping the traditional areas of personnel management, industrial relations, organisational behaviour, and strategic and operational management. Many proponents of HRM argue that it addresses the centrality of employees in the organisation, and that their motivation and commitment to organisational goals need to be nurtured. While this is by no means a new concept, the HRM perspective would suggest that a range of organisational objectives have been arranged in a strategic way to enhance the performance of employees in achieving these goals.

A construction project in the built environment will involve many skilled professionals and manual labourers. Management needs to co-ordinate different professionals, construction companies and supplier companies, whose involvement can change throughout the duration of the project. The nature of the construction industry and the need to integrate various construction professionals gives the built environment a complex project-related culture in which good HRM practices need to be adopted. There are factors, such as economic and technological change, which have an effect on all industries; however, there are specific issues that affect the way HR is managed in companies in the built environment, including:

- *One-off projects*—for example, the end product of a public contract may be a school, which will be expected to last for many years without being replaced.
- *Contracts awarded at short notice*—a contractor who has been awarded a project at short notice will have to arrange their resources and employees quickly in order to met the project's requirements.
- *Temporary project teams and workers who move between different sites*—the composition of the project team can also change over the course of a project.
- *Client pressure*—over time extra effort may be required by the project team to satisfy the client's needs.
- *A male-dominated workforce*—although the number of women working in the built environment has increased, it is still perceived as being a male-dominated industry. This has an impact on the human resource policies adopted by companies.
- *Skills required by employees will change*—for example, more sophisticated technologies require employees to be upskilled and re-skilled.

8.3 Hard and soft HRM

Legge's (1995) review of the literature on personnel and HRM identified problems with 'hard' and 'soft' HRM. Hard HRM emphasises the term *resource* and views people as another economic factor and a cost that must be controlled. The business needs of the organisation suggest that human resources will be acquired, used and dispensed with as corporate planning requires. Hard HRM pays little attention to the needs of those human resources. Hard HRM is sometimes defined in terms of the particular policies that stress a cost-minimisation strategy with an emphasis on leanness in production, and the use of labour as a resource in the employment relationship. For many years companies in the built environment adopted a hard HRM approach: managers were primarily concerned with cost and production. However, there has been a shift away from this style in recent years.

Soft HRM focuses on the term *human* and emphasises the importance of training and development, enabling better-skilled employees to give a competitive advantage to their organisation. The human aspects also suggest that all employees (regardless of grade) should be developed and that the behavioural aspects of people at work should be considered to be of the utmost importance. Soft HRM also views the employee as being integrated into a work process that values trust, commitment and communication. Increasing numbers of organisations in the built environment are acknowledging that a softer approach to HRM will contribute to organisational success. This is evident in the increased use of training and development programmes by construction companies for the benefit of both employees and the entire company.

8.4 Human resource management activities

HRM activities vary from one organisation to another and are affected by the size and structure of an organisation. In general, the activities performed by a human resource manager may be divided into the following areas:
- staffing
- employee development
- performance management
- employee relations
- rewards
- employee maintenance.

Staffing

Traditionally, human resource managers spent a great deal of time recruiting and selecting employees. Employment patterns, however, are changing, and changing work methods give rise to requirements for different and new skills and for existing employees to be more flexible in adapting to new working methods. Hiring staff on an ad hoc basis puts the continuity and development of all employees at risk. The recruitment, selection and promotion of employees are expensive processes and are often difficult to reverse if errors are made. To deal with these variables, human resource planning is needed to analyse current employee needs and to prepare an organisation for future requirements. One of the primary functions of human resource planning is to estimate what numbers of people and what skills are required to achieve organisational goals. A human resource plan should present a detailed analysis of staffing requirements for an organisation and should include a statement on how vacancies are to be filled. Human resource planning, therefore, is the starting point for establishing an organisation's human resource strategy, as this planning seeks to integrate the operations of an organisation with the skills of a labour force in order to satisfy customer demands.

Human resource planning in the built environment aims to ensure that there will be a sufficient supply of appropriately skilled labour. Analysing future workloads and labour requirements can be difficult because of the current economic crisis in the industry.

Human resource planning addresses issues such as:

- *Accommodation*—Is there a need for more or fewer rooms, desks, etc?
- *Costs*—Where is there a need for additional/fewer resources?
- *Culture*—How are changes going to affect the way people interact?
- *Development*—Will there be different opportunities for staff development?
- *Industrial relations*—How will trade unions react to changes?
- *Organisation development*—Do reporting relationships need to be changed or reorganised?
- *Promotion*—What opportunities for individual advancement will there be?
- *Recruitment*—What number and sort of people will need to be recruited?
- *Redundancy*—Which groups are likely to face redundancy and how is this going to be dealt with?
- *Reward systems*—Should financial and non-financial rewards be revised?
- *Training and re-training*—Which groups need to develop new skills?
- *Working practices*—Is there a need to rethink the ways in which tasks are addressed?

A human resource plan illustrates the number of employees that an organisation will need for the next stage in the staffing function—the recruitment process.

The recruitment process

The major stages of the recruitment process are:
- job analysis, job descriptions and person specifications
- advertising
- administration of recruitment.

Job analysis consists of data about each job, what activities are to be performed, and what skills are needed. Job analysis will often involve the use of job descriptions (Figure 8.1) and person specifications (Figure 8.2).

Job descriptions usually include the following elements:
- job title
- rates of pay
- grade
- location
- department
- job summary—a brief statement of why the job exists
- job content—a list of the main duties to be performed
- reporting structure
- miscellaneous details, for example shift work and car allowance.

Figure 8.1 Sample job description

Job Title:	**Project Quantity Surveyor**
Salary:	An attractive salary and package available to the successful candidate
Location:	Mid-West Regional Office
Department:	Government Projects
Reports to:	Regional Director
Responsible for:	Quantity Surveying services for public sector projects
Main Duties:	● Planning and control of capital costs under the Irish Government's Capital Works Management Framework (CWMF).
	● Leading a project quantity surveying team of chartered surveyors, graduates and undergraduate placements.
	● Full range of professional quantity surveying services.

Person specifications outline the knowledge, skills and personal qualities a person will require in order to be able to perform the tasks outlined in a job description. The following elements are commonly included in person specifications:
- physical make-up—any necessary and justifiable (that is, non-discriminatory in equality/legislation terms) physical requirements which are essential to the job
- qualifications, education, training and experience
- personal qualities, for example good written and oral communication skills, confidence, dependability
- motivation, such as high expectations of self and others.

Figure 8.2 Sample person specification

Job Title:	**Project Quantity Surveyor**
Department:	Government Projects
Qualifications:	Honours degree in Quantity Surveying, Chartered Member of the Society of Chartered Surveyors or the Royal Institution of Chartered Surveyors
Experience:	Minimum of five years' experience in a professional quantity surveying organisation at project surveyor level.
Knowledge and Skills:	● Expert knowledge of the Irish Government's Capital Works Management Framework (CWMF).
	● Knowledge of the full range of professional quantity surveying services.
	● Excellent management and leadership skills.
Personal Qualities:	● Self-motivated, ethical, professional communicator with excellent interpersonal skills.

Administration of recruitment

Recruitment is the business of attracting sufficient suitable candidates for the job at a reasonable cost. The administration of the recruitment process is usually done by the personnel/HRM department. This involves placing advertisements, sending application forms and job descriptions to potential candidates, and receiving the completed forms. The advantage of the personnel/HRM department in dealing with the administration of recruitment is that consistency between departments can exist, with a corporate approach for differing posts. There are various methods of recruiting people, including:

- internal advertising
- newspaper advertisements
- radio, TV and cinema advertising
- word of mouth
- local schools, colleges and universities
- recruitment consultants
- recruitment fairs
- the Internet
- specialist and professional papers and journals
- job centres
- headhunting.

The best method is the one that produces the most suitable candidates at a reasonable cost.

Most third-level colleges in Ireland hold recruitment fairs. Companies in the built environment view these as occasions on which to recruit graduates and work placement students. The annual built environment recruitment fair in Limerick Institute of Technology, for example, normally attracts over seventy construction companies including contractors, civil engineers, quantity surveyors and real estate companies. Companies are given an opportunity to meet students face to face and arrange further interviews with students they believe are suited to their company.

In the current economic climate, recruitment of staff in the built environment tends to be through word of mouth and headhunting. Construction companies that are attempting to keep their costs down do not wish to incur the expense of using advertising or recruitment companies. Generally, companies will also have a number of CVs on file, which they would have received from various skilled people seeking work as a result of being made redundant.

The selection process

Once an organisation's advertisement has attracted a manageable number of suitably qualified and/or experienced individuals, the human resource manager must decide on the best way to select interested candidates. Table 8.1 identifies a number of selection methods available to managers.

Table 8.1 Selection methods and the selection process

Selection Methods	Selection Process
Application forms	Application forms provide the basic information needed for an initial trawl prior to short-listing. The forms need to be designed for easy use, with the opportunity for individuals to offer additional material where they want.
CVs	Curricula vitae (CVs) are similar to application forms, except that the candidates select their own ways of presenting the data about themselves and their careers.
Interviews	Interviews remain popular because they offer an opportunity for face-to-face conversation. They also allow for comparison between candidates.
Tests	Tests, for example aptitude, personality and selection tests, which relate to the skills necessary to do the job. It is important that a prescribed test really does test the skills that are needed to do the job and does not discriminate unfairly.
Assessment centres	Assessment centres (assessment of several candidates together by several observers using a variety of selection methods, for example psychological tests, team-building exercises, structured discussions and role-playing exercises). The value lies in the variety of evidence collected; but assessment centres are expensive to run, both in time and money, so are usually reserved for senior appointments such as chief executives.

The ultimate goal of selection is often expressed as *choosing the best person for the job*. The objectives of the selection process, therefore, are to:
*   gather as much relevant information as possible
*   assess each candidate in order to forecast performance on the job
*   give information to applicants so that they can judge whether or not they would wish to accept an offer of employment.

An organisation may decide to use a variety of selection methods, for example supplementing interviews with psychological tests and personality questionnaires, depending on the vacancy to be filled.

Interviews are the most common method of selection used in the built environment. After the first interview, some candidates are often invited to attend a second interview until the most suitable candidate is selected.

Employee development

A definition of employee development is:

> The skilful provision and organisation of learning experiences in the workplace so that performance can be improved, work goals can be achieved, and that—through enhancing the skills, knowledge, learning ability and enthusiasm at

every level—there can be continuous organisational as well as individual growth. Employee development must, therefore, be part of a wider strategy for the business, aligned with the organisation's corporate mission and goals (Harrison 2000).

Employee development relates to employees acquiring a broad range of skills through planned activities and experience, and is concerned with an individual's overall career development rather than training for his/her current role. To support staff development, the human resource manager engages in:

- analysing training requirements
- appraising employee performance
- developing employee career plans
- encouraging employee involvement
- providing development opportunities
- providing employee counselling
- improving employee welfare.

Individual employees may attend management courses, participate in job rotation, committees and special projects or train as understudies to various senior managers. The human resource manager needs to assess the type of training that will benefit the organisation as well as each individual employee. Training and development may be conducted on the job, for example job instruction, coaching, job rotation, and participation in special projects and assignments. Alternatively, off-the-job training may be used, for example seminar/workshop attendance, role-playing and guided reading.

Appraising employee performance is another mechanism for employee development as it concerns making judgments about employees' past performance. Employee appraisals can be used to improve current performance by providing feedback on strengths and weaknesses. Performance appraisals should be linked to a performance improvement process, which can be used to identify training needs and to focus on career plans and career development. Appraisals can be effective for increasing employee motivation, which in turn increases organisational performance. The performance appraisal interview provides time for an employee and manager to discuss an employee's progress in his or her current position, as well as discussing opportunities for progression within the organisation. A concern for employee welfare is also a function of the human resource manager. This function includes:

- ensuring that health and safety legislation is enforced
- maintaining good employee relations
- providing counselling (that is, helping people to help themselves)
- providing an employee assistance programme (EAP).

Many different issues can be dealt with by an EAP, for example alcohol abuse, verbal abuse, racial harassment, retirement, marital problems, disability, gambling, bereavement, financial advice, literacy, Aids and other medical issues, redundancy, legal matters, divorce (Berridge and Cooper 1994). If employee development is successfully designed and managed, it can contribute to the success of the organisation within the contemporary business environment.

Many professional companies in the built environment encourage their employees to become chartered in their chosen profession. Additionally, companies support employees with training and development opportunities to help employees in their continuing professional development, which in turn will add extra benefit to the company. Table 8.2 illustrates the employee development practices that John Sisk & Sons Ltd (Ireland's largest general contracting company) has in place for their employees.

Table 8.2 Employee development practices adopted by Sisk Ltd (www.sisk.ie)

Training and Development	Description
Fourth-level education	• Professional development programmes have been established for all professional disciplines. • In committing to these programmes, the company ensures that the employee's career will be enhanced with a broad range of experience which will be regularly supported by training on site and at office-based training facilities. • Programmes are generally split into three levels, and on graduating from one level to another, employees will gain further responsibilities that reflect their increased capability. • Having actively participated in a development programme will ensure that the employee becomes recognised as a highly experienced, effective and respected professional within the company and industry alike.
Mentoring	• To ensure that the company meets its commitments, employees will be assigned a mentor who will initially assist employees in settling into their role. • While participating in a programme, employees will meet their mentor on a regular basis, who will guide and assist them in progressing through their development programme.
Management skills development	• As staff progress and develop within the company, they will begin to assume greater responsibilities at management level. To support this progression, the company provides extensive soft skills and management development programmes to support and assist staff in these challenging roles. • These programmes include seminars and courses ranging from managing safety on site to courses in report writing and time management. The programmes provide a wide variety of opportunities to develop the skills necessary to succeed in a management position within Sisk.
Further education and sponsorship	• Recognising the ambition of staff to develop their careers in the industry, the company sponsors a significant number of further education courses.

	• Courses which Sisk have sponsored in the past include Higher Diploma in Project Management, MSc in Building Services Technology, Cleanroom Technology and Construction, and Higher Diploma in Contract Law.
Apprenticeships	• Since the company's establishment in 1859, John Sisk & Son Ltd has been training apprentices in many trades, and more recently in Carpentry and Joinery, and Blocklaying.
	• The company fully supports the four-year Apprentice training programme and recruits annually for its Dublin-based Carpentry and Joinery Training Centre.
	• The training centre is the only one of its kind in the country, and is responsible for the development of highly skilled carpenters, who in the past have won the esteemed Apprentice of the Year Award on many occasions.
	• For apprentices who successfully complete the programme, and who have demonstrated outstanding commitment, Sisk provides them with the opportunity to participate in a Foreman Development Programme, which introduces them to a challenging and rewarding career in site management.

Performance management

Performance management is an established way of providing feedback, guidance and monitoring for employees. The assessment process in performance management is linked to job definitions and is rigorous and objective. It is based on organisational objective-setting and individual development plans and it is sometimes linked with financial rewards. In many systems, an element of self-appraisal is also included. Some of the reasons why managers might want to appraise their staff include:

• human resource considerations—to ensure that the abilities and energies of employees are being used effectively. Managers would hope to find out more about their employees and to make better use of each individual's talents and expertise

• training—to identify training needs for new tasks and to improve poor performance among employees

• promotion—talking to employees about their aspirations as well as finding out about their performance can assist decision-making about who is ready for promotion

• planning—to identify skill shortages and succession needs.

Performance management is usually taken to mean an increased emphasis on specifying what is wanted and rewarding those employees who are able to deliver it satisfactorily. An employee working in the built environment might work on different project teams throughout a year under the guidance of a supervisor. The immediate supervisor would be the most appropriate person to undertake the employee appraisal.

Performance management is also applicable to the management of a construction project. Balancing the aims of a company with the particular aims of employees is more likely to make the company more efficient. Companies can use key performance indicators when analysing the performance being achieved on a construction project. These indicators include:

- health and safety
- employee satisfaction
- staff turnover
- absenteeism
- working hours
- qualifications and skills.

Employee relations

Employee relations includes negotiations between management and union representatives (in a union environment) and dealing with disciplinary procedures and grievances. In any organisation, there will be occasions when problems or difficulties occur between management and employees. In order that these problems do not turn into bigger issues, suitable ways of dealing with them are devised to resolve them. If a problem arises from a particular activity, or inactivity, of management, this may result in an employee having a grievance. Grievance procedures exist to enable employees to have formal means of complaint about their employment terms and conditions, working environment and related issues. Table 8.3 lists some trade unions that represent employees in the built environment in Ireland.

If a problem arises from the behaviour or attitude of an employee, disciplinary action may be called for. Disciplinary rules set the standards of workplace behaviour. Generally, these rules refer to overall conduct, health and safety, security, time-keeping and attendance. Disciplinary rules help to ensure a consistent and fair approach to the treatment of employees. Breaches of disciplinary rules vary in their seriousness; for example, a minor infringement, such as occasional late arrival at work, might merit an oral warning which might not be formally recorded, whereas more serious infringements might prompt written warnings. Gross misconduct can result in dismissal, for example because of theft or drug misuse in the workplace.

In a unionised environment, trade unions pursue a common interest with management in promoting standards of conduct by all. By representing their members, their role is to promote and protect their members' rights.

Table 8.3 Trade unions in the built environment

Trade Union	Summary
Services, Industrial, Professional and Technical Union (SIPTU) www.siptu.ie	• SIPTU represents a wide range of workers in the construction industry including crane drivers, scaffolders, steel fixers, plant operatives, painters and others. • As a result of the union's efforts in organising construction workers, minimum rates of pay, terms and conditions of employment, pension and sick pay schemes are legally binding in the industry for all workers, irrespective of their nationality. • SIPTU is also widely acknowledged as the driving force behind the ongoing campaign to secure proper health and safety standards for building workers in Ireland.

Building and Allied Trades Union (BATU) www.batu.i	• Represents around 9,000 workers in the building industry, including:
	  • brick and stone layers
	  • carpenters and joiners
	  • stonecutters
	  • wood cutting machinists
	in addition to apprentices to the above trades.
	• Aims are to develop the union's website into a useful tool for information for members and construction workers in general.
	• Intends to demonstrate and promote the wide diversity of skills and talent of its members and to provide news and updates on developments within members' trades.

Union of Construction Allied Trades and Technicians (UCATT) Ireland www.ucatt.ie	• UCATT represents over 15,000 craft workers in Ireland and is dedicated to improving the working conditions of building workers. • Is at the forefront of negotiations concerning members' pay, terms and conditions of employment, whether members are employed in local authorities, health boards, government departments or the construction industry.

Rewards

Human resource managers design and administer appropriate reward systems, evaluate jobs, decide on benefits and ensure fair treatment for all employees. There are a number of words which are used to describe what an employee receives in return for his/her work efforts.

- Benefits—the non-cash elements of an employee's reward package, for example a paid holiday.
- Compensation—payment for work performed, injuries received or loss of employment (i.e. pay and benefits).
- Salary—a financial reward for work done and usually received on a monthly basis.
- Wages—a financial reward for work done and usually received on a weekly basis (generally associated with manual workers).

Reward packages can include financial and non-financial rewards:
- employee share options
- payments for medical insurance and pensions
- childcare
- assistance for further education
- a company car.

In the built environment, overtime is the most common form of additional reward for employees. When a project is running over budget or schedule, employees will need to work extra hours to complete the project. Offering to pay overtime is a good incentive for construction workers both on site and in offices as they are being rewarded for their extra effort. Financial rewards are typically used in the built environment, and during the boom years non-financial rewards were increasingly offered to employees, for example car park spaces, office spaces and promotion.

An effective reward system has four main characteristics.
1. The reward system must meet the needs of the employee for basic necessities. These needs include the physiological and security needs identified by Maslow and the hygiene factors identified by Herzberg.
2. The rewards should compare favourably with those offered by other organisations. Unfavourable comparisons with people in other settings could result in feelings of inequity.
3. The distribution of rewards within the organisation must be equitable. When some employees believe they are underpaid in comparison with others in the organisation, the probable results are low morale and poor performance.
4. The reward system must recognise that different people have different needs and that people choose different paths to satisfy those needs. Insofar as possible, a variety of rewards and a variety of methods for satisfying needs should be made available to employees.

Marchington and Wilkinson (2000) suggest that employers need to turn their attention to non-financial rewards in the form of recognition, appreciation and feedback for their employees. Other valuable non-financial rewards are job-design initiatives to make work more satisfying and fulfilling and the provision of variety, involvement, autonomy and responsibility. Given the large cost to an organisation of reward packages, it is important that managers assess the benefit that accrues to the organisation because of those packages. An organisation must provide reasonable pay and appropriate benefits to its employees; however, it is in the best interest of the organisation that its resources are managed wisely. As part of the recruiting process, it is necessary for the organisation to be seen as an attractive employer in order to hire high-quality human resources. The attractiveness of an organisation as an employer is a function, in part, of the total compensation package, which includes employee benefits.

Employee maintenance

Employee maintenance includes the provision of equal opportunities, the monitoring of workplace health and safety policies, and staff retention endeavours. Human resource managers need to be familiar with legislation and their organisation's policies in relation to women, disabled people, people from ethnic minorities and other sectors.

Health and safety policies are now statutory requirements for all employers since the introduction of the Safety, Health and Welfare at Work (Construction) Regulations 2006. The main items covered under health and safety legislation are:

- arrangements for emergencies
- safety provision on construction sites
- reporting of incidents and injuries
- recording of accidents
- the provision and use of safe working equipment.

Figure 8.3 illustrates examples of the safety signs that are generally used on construction sites. Construction sites can be dangerous environments due to the height of buildings and large volumes of machinery being used. A Safe Pass card is a certification that all construction workers must hold by law in order to work on a construction site. The Safe Pass aims to ensure that all construction workers will have a basic knowledge of health and safety, and be able to work on-site without being a risk to themselves or others who might be affected by their acts or omissions.

Figure 8.3 Examples of site safety signs used on construction sites

Human resource managers in the built environment must now manage human resources in a declining market. While companies adjust their business models to reflect a smaller number of building projects, managers must ensure that the core skill sets and human resources that the organisation needs are retained, and that those members of staff who must leave the organisation are given assistance. Staff who are let go from organisations may receive redundancy payments but would much rather be employed in their chosen careers. Human resource managers can bring a great deal of transition knowledge and skills to employees in terms of helping them to:

• assess their skill sets
• review options for further training and education
• explore potential career changes
• adjust work–life balance
• understand their social security entitlements
• be aware of future opportunities within the organisation when the upturn comes.

8.5 Key points

The concept of human resource management (HRM) and the use of the term grew and developed during the 1980s and 1990s. Its conceptual origin can be traced back to the 1890s, when the human resource manager or personnel practitioner was involved with welfare work. HRM differs from traditional personnel management activities as it is concerned with the *integration of employees* in all departments of an organisation working towards the achievement of common goals. HRM also takes a *strategic perspective* on recruiting and developing employees and emphasises the importance of the manager as leader, together with devolving and delegating power to supervisors (line managers). The activities of human resource managers have now shifted from the original narrow focus of welfare work to issues related to the acquisition, development and maintenance of human resources in an organisation. HRM varies depending on the size, structure and culture of an organisation. There are, however, a number of HRM activities common to all organisations, including:

• human resource planning
• recruitment and selection of employees
• managing employee relations
• rewarding employees
• employee development
• retaining employees.

Important terms and concepts

development programme (p. 132)
employee development (p. 136)
employee maintenance (p. 143)
employee relations (p. 140)

Questions for review

1. Describe the background to human resource management (HRM).
2. Detail the main functions performed by human resource managers in organisations.
3. Differentiate between hard and soft HRM.
4. Evaluate the contribution of the human resource manager to the success of an organisation, citing examples from an organisation in the built environment.
5. Describe the recruitment and selection process for an organisation in the built environment.
6. What advice would you offer a firm of quantity surveyors planning to recruit a project quantity surveyor for their regional office?
7. Discuss organisational rewards in the context of some of the motivational theories with which you are familiar.
8. How can human resource managers help built environment employees who are facing redundancy?

9
STRATEGIC MANAGEMENT

Learning outcomes

Following study of this chapter you will be able to:
- recognise the steps in a strategic management process
- identify various levels of strategy
- understand portfolio management techniques
- explain strategic human resource management.

9.1 Strategy defined

Strategy can be defined as an action plan for the future to accomplish organisational goals. An action plan should address questions such as what to do and how to do it. Strategy is a planning activity that top managers perform to provide long-term direction and scope to an organisation (see Chapter 3). Strategy also achieves *advantage* for the organisation by its uses of *resources* within a changing *environment*. Porter (1996) states that an essential element of strategy is choosing what *not* to do, which is as important as choosing what to do.

Strategic management is a way of approaching business opportunities and challenges, and is a comprehensive and ongoing management process aimed at formulating and implementing effective strategies (Griffin 2008). Strategic management includes the maintenance of a 'vision of the future' that is constantly updated by data on both internal and external environments (Aktouf 1996). At its simplest, strategic management can be described as a plan of action that enables an organisation to move from where it is now to where it wants to be in the future. Strategic management, therefore, is an ongoing process influenced by:
- senior management
- input from line managers
- the environment
- resources.

Strategic management is concerned with complexity arising out of ambiguous and non-routine situations with organisation-wide rather than operation-wide implications. Strategic management also involves making strategic choices for the future and turning strategy into action. Strategic management in the built environment can involve a construction company deciding to expand into other, areas of construction, for example a building contractor diversifying into civil engineering work such as road construction. It may also involve working with a different client or location, for example a quantity surveying company working predominantly in the private sector may decide to seek projects in the public sector and tender for buildings such as schools and public hospitals.

Strategic management differs in nature and scope from operational management because of its:

- ambiguous/uncertain nature
- complexity
- organisation-wide focus
- long-term implications

Operational management:

- is routinised
- is operationally specific
- is short-term
- deals with day-to-day activities of supervisors such as site managers on construction sites.

In general, a well-conceived strategy addresses three areas.

1. Distinctive competence—something the organisation does exceptionally well. Murray O'Laoire Architects, for example, won two Royal Institute of Architects of Ireland (RIAI) awards for Best Educational Building in 2008, highlighting their ability to design educational buildings.
2. Scope—the part of a strategy that specifies the range of markets in which an organisation will compete. If a construction company is expanding, the scope would be related to the new area the company intends to enter, for example housing, civil infrastructure, wind farms, etc.
3. Resource deployment—how an organisation distributes its resources across the areas in which it competes. A quantity surveying practice, for example, may have employees with qualifications in both quantity surveying and project management. This allows the company to bid for not only quantity surveying work but also project management projects.

9.2 The strategic management process

The strategic management process may be divided into five steps.

Step 1: Organisational direction

The first step in the strategic management process begins with senior managers evaluating an organisation's position in relation to the organisation's *mission* and *goals.* As described in Chapter 3, a mission is an organisation's reason for existing and indicates the future direction that senior management has for the organisation. A goal is a desired future state that the organisation attempts to realise (Daft 1998).

Objectives are clear and explicit and there is careful and thorough analysis of the internal and external factors that might affect the organisation's strategic direction. The structure of the organisation should be suited to the strategy to be followed; and the various control systems, such as budgets and management by objectives, should facilitate organisational direction. These controls provide means by which senior management can assess whether people in the organisation are meeting expected objectives and if the strategic direction of the organisation is being attained.

Applying organisational direction to a construction project can be interpreted as deciding on appropriate goals and objectives at the beginning of the project process and evaluating their progress during the construction process. This can help increase the overall quality of construction and the likelihood of on-time completion.

Step 2: Environmental analysis

Environmental analysis involves looking at the internal *strengths* and *weaknesses* of an organisation together with the *opportunities* and *threats* posed by the *external* environment.

This is often referred to as a **SWOT analysis**. SWOT stands for:

*   Strengths
*   Weaknesses
*   Opportunities
*   Threats.

Strengths and weaknesses—*internal environmental analysis*—tend to concentrate on the present and past; opportunities and threats—*external environmental analysis*—usually refer to the present and future of an organisation.

Organisational strengths are skills and capabilities that enable an organisation to conceive and implement its strategies. A **distinctive competence** is a strength possessed by an organisation. A main purpose of SWOT analysis is to discover an organisation's distinctive competencies so that the organisation can choose and implement strategies that exploit its unique organisational strengths. A general construction company that has an employee with expertise in timber-framed house building may use a SWOT analysis to highlight opportunities and threats involved in diversifying into this new market. Table 9.1 highlights issues that need to be considered for a SWOT analysis for a construction company in the built environment.

Organisational weaknesses are skills and capabilities that do not enable an organisation to choose and implement strategies that support its objectives. An organisation has essentially two ways of addressing weaknesses. First, it may need to make investments to obtain the strengths required to implement strategies that support its mission. Second, the organisation may need to modify its mission so that it can be accomplished with the skills and capabilities that the organisation already possesses.

Organisational opportunities are areas in the environment that, if exploited, may generate high performance. **Organisational threats** are areas in the environment that increase the difficulty for an organisation in achieving high performance. In some cases, what can be seen as a strength in one organisation may be considered a threat to another. The economic climate and the environment in which the organisation operates need to be taken into account when analysing a company's strengths and weaknesses.

Table 9.1 Issues to be considered in a SWOT analysis of a construction company

Strengths and Weaknesses	Opportunities and Threats
Financial standing	New markets
Competitive advantage	Existing customers
Public perception	Competition
Strategic direction	Economic recession
Facilities	Labour availability/redundancies
Management expertise	Suppliers' workload
Market leader	Expansion of the EU
Cost advantages	Inflation levels
Reputation for quality	Terrorism and war
Reputation for completion on time	Mergers and takeovers
Construction expertise	Location of business
Employee turnover	Employment legislation
Land bank	Sub-contractors' workload
Morale of employees	Risk

Step 3: Strategy formulation

Strategy formulation involves senior managers *gathering relevant information to determine future actions of an organisation*. This process suggests that, from a SWOT analysis (Step 2), managers have to make decisions or *strategic choices* to enable their organisation to meet its goals. Strategies are formulated at corporate (top), business (middle) and functional (lower) levels (see section 9.3 Levels of strategy). There is no one right way in which strategy is formulated: for example, strategies which are formulated in a fast-changing environment are not likely to be the same as in an environment in which there is little change. Typically, strategy formulation is written about as though it is developed by managers in an intended, planned fashion.

Intended strategy is an expression of desired strategic direction deliberately formulated or planned by managers. Often organisations use an **emergent strategy**—a pattern of action that develops over time from within the organisation rather than from the top down. Strategy *emerges* from innovation and from the variety and diversity which exist in and around organisations.

Step 4: Strategy implementation

Strategy implementation involves *the activities that are required to put strategies into action*. It focuses on the processes through which strategies are achieved, for example structure, leadership, and control systems. This step focuses on *how* the strategy is to be achieved.

In many organisations, however, the attempt to follow detailed intended strategies is only partially achieved in practice. The intended strategy is, therefore, replaced by a realised strategy. A **realised strategy** is the strategy actually being followed by an organisation in practice. There are various reasons for this, such as: the plans are unworkable; the environment changes after the strategy has been drawn up and the managers decide that the strategy, as planned, should not be put into effect; or people in the organisation or influential stakeholders do not go along with the strategy.

Step 5: Strategy evaluation

Strategy evaluation determines whether *actual* change and performance is taking place and whether or not the change matches the *desired* change and performance.

9.3 Levels of strategy

Strategy is generally formulated at three levels:
- corporate
- business
- functional.

Corporate-level strategy

Corporate-level strategy describes an organisation's overall direction. It is concerned with the question *What business should we be in?* It considers the combination of businesses in terms of markets, products and nations. In the case of large organisations, it looks at the management of its various business units. A strategic business unit (SBU) is a unit of a company that has a separate mission and separate objectives, and can be planned independently from other company businesses. Large organisations develop separate business-level strategies for each of their divisions or units, each of which might be engaged in producing very different products or services. In the case of smaller organisations, corporate and business-level strategies may be combined.

Corporate-level strategy may be viewed as a grand plan for an organisation which describes the general actions to be taken to achieve long-term objectives. A grand strategy represents the overall direction a business intends to follow. Senior managers may choose from three grand strategy options (Table 9.2):
- retrenchment
- stability
- growth

Table 9.2 Grand strategy options for a housing developer

Grand Strategy	Characteristics	Action	Reason for Implementation
Retrenchment	Cutting back on range of products or markets.	Curtailment of speculative apartment development.	Management recognises that its organisation is performing badly.
Stability	Continuing with the same products and markets.	Maintaining production level of one-off housing units.	Management recognises that its organisation is performing well and opts for low risk and little change in a stable environment.
Growth	Seeking to add new products and new markets	Converting NAMA-based* developments into social and affordable housing units.	Management wants its organisation to perform much better, preferring high risk and change.

* NAMA is the National Asset Management Agency for non-performing property developments with Irish-based banking finance

A **retrenchment strategy** is implemented by an organisation if senior management decides to reduce an organisation's size in terms of employees, production or assets. This may be the result of a decline in demand for an organisation's products, the introduction of new technology, or increased competition. Retrenchment usually involves selling off parts of a business or even the liquidation of an entire organisation. The majority of construction companies and design consultancies pursue aggressive retrenchment strategies during periods of recession.

A **stability strategy** involves an organisation's attempt to remain the same size or to grow in a very slow, controlled way. This strategy may be implemented after a period of rapid growth in order to 'take stock' and ensure that the expansion is viable. Construction companies with long-term experience of 'boom and bust' cycles tend to stabilise their organisation by organising their staff and resources in a particular manner, for example:
- only essential personnel are offered full-time employment; all other staff are employed on a temporary or contract basis
- the head office is purchased; all other offices are rented.

During a recession, contract staff might not be renewed if work is unavailable; surplus rented office accommodation might be vacated; and the full-time critical mass of staff and resources could be maintained until activity in the economy improves.

A construction company may also refocus its business model into a safer niche market segment to ensure the stability of the organisation during a period of recession.

A **growth strategy** involves an organisation developing its market position through increased investment, new product development, and diversification into new markets, for example foreign markets, to encourage expansion. This is an easy strategy to implement in boom periods; however, in the long term, property development companies implement this strategy in periods of recession by acquiring development land and/or failed developments at reduced prices and either re-financing the development or holding it until the market has recovered.

Business-level strategy

Business-level strategy is concerned with the question *How do we succeed in this particular business?* Porter (1980) proposed three business strategies, known as Porter's generic strategies (see Chapter 2). A second classification of business-level strategy was developed by Miles and Snow (1978). These authors suggested that a business-level strategy usually fits into one of four categories (Table 9.3):

- defender strategies
- prospector strategies
- analyser strategies
- reactor strategies.

Table 9.3 Miles and Snow's business strategies

Strategy	Definition	Example
Defender	Focuses on existing customers, maintains stable growth	One-off houses
Prospector	Focuses on innovation and growth, encourages risk taking	Wind farm contractor
Analyser	Focuses on maintaining current markets with moderate innovation in new markets	Civil engineering contractor
Reactor	No clear strategy, reacts to changes in the environment	Small works contractor: extensions, conversions, energy/insulation

According to Miles and Snow, an organisation that implements a **defender strategy** has a limited product line and its management focus is on improving the efficiency of existing operations. This strategy concentrates on protecting current market share, maintaining stable growth and serving current customers.

An organisation that implements a **prospector strategy** focuses on new product development, innovation and market opportunities and typically has a number of product lines. Such an organisation would be constantly expanding into new markets and would also be a high risk taker.

An organisation that implements an **analyser strategy** generally operates in at least two different markets, one stable (thus protecting existing operations) and one variable (thus creating new market opportunities). Managers in these organisations emphasise efficiency in the stable market and innovation in the variable market.

An organisation that implements a **reactor strategy** has no consistent strategic approach. Such a company fails to anticipate environmental changes and usually responds to these changes only in a piecemeal fashion.

Functional-level Strategy

Functional-level strategy is concerned with the ongoing functional operations of an organisation. The functions represented in an organisation depend on the type of business, its size and its structure, but may include marketing, sales, research and development, finance and human resources. Strategy at the functional level addresses the question *How do we support the business-level competitive strategy?* All these functions need to follow the strategic plans of an organisation and must be integrated to ensure the overall success of an organisation.

9.4 The corporate portfolio

Every organisation consists of at least one and usually many more products and services. These products or services represent the *business portfolio*; for example, in the pre-cast concrete manufacturing industry there are a wide range of pre-cast products produced by each manufacturer. An organisation can be regarded as a 'portfolio' of businesses which its managers balance by expanding investment in some while reducing investment in others. Managers have to decide on the investment of resources in their various businesses. Most organisations like to have a balanced mix of business units which are at different stages in their life cycles. For construction companies, different departments such as estimating and tendering will have projects that are at different stages of planning, construction or completion, all of which are part of the company's portfolio.

Portfolio management techniques are methods that organisations with many business units use to determine which businesses to engage in and how to manage these businesses in order to maximise corporate performance. Two well-known portfolio management techniques are:
- the Boston Consulting Group matrix
- the General Electric Business Screen.

The Boston Consulting Group (BCG) matrix

The use of the BCG matrix helps managers to define:
* What business should we be in?
* What is our basic mission?
* How should we allocate corporate resources across the various business units?

The matrix analyses businesses along two dimensions:
* business growth
* market share.

The business growth dimension measures how rapidly a whole industry is increasing in size, while market share measures the share a business unit has of this market in comparison to its competitors' share. By assessing each strategic business unit (SBU) on the basis of its market growth rate and relative market share, managers can make decisions about committing further financial resources to an SBU or, instead, to sell or liquidate an SBU.

Once managers have determined the growth rate of a market and the particular product or service market share, it is then possible to allocate each business unit to one of four quadrants in the matrix (see Figure 9.1). The allocation of individual business units to a particular position on the matrix should help managers to define strategic plans for a business that are consistent with corporate strategy. The matrix classifies the types of businesses that a diversified organisation can engage in; in this case, dogs, cash cows, question marks and stars.

Figure 9.1 The Boston Consulting Group (BCG) matrix

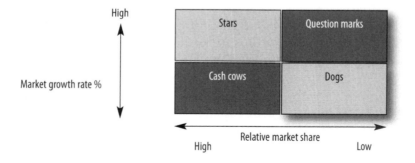

Organisations may want to have a number of business units in each quadrant, with a number of products and services producing a cash flow among other businesses requiring an injection of cash.

Stars, according to the BCG matrix, are businesses that have the largest share of a rapidly growing market. Cash generated by cash cows should be invested in stars as they represent the best opportunities for future growth and survival. Stars are important because, as well as being successful, they have potential for further expansion. As a star's industry becomes more mature and growth slows, less investment will be required and the star will transform itself into a cash cow.

Question marks are businesses that have only a small share of a quickly growing market. The future performance of these particular businesses is uncertain and risky. The BCG matrix suggests that organisations should invest carefully in question marks. Investment might develop some into stars, while other question marks may fail regardless of investment. The BCG matrix suggests that an organisation should have some question marks in its portfolio as potential future stars.

Cash cows are businesses that have a large share of a market that is not expected to grow substantially. These businesses generate high profits and the excess cash they produce may be used for investment in question marks and stars. Low investment in cash cows means that these businesses should be profitable and they should also generate surplus cash as they age. From the corporate point of view, cash cows can be 'milked' to provide funds for investment in newer riskier businesses.

Dogs are businesses that have a very small share of a market that is not expected to grow. Dogs represent weak businesses and the BCG matrix suggests that organisations should not invest in these businesses or should consider selling them.

The BCG matrix has been criticised because of the difficulty in using it to describe accurately some products or services and business units; for example, the marginal difference between divesting in a question mark with potential for growth and development of a star may be very small. It may be based on an estimation of market growth and the potential for future growth. Another criticism of the matrix is that it may be too narrowly focused; for example, other factors besides market growth and market share can determine the performance of a business. Despite its weaknesses, however, the portfolio concept still exists in organisations, but it tends to help debate rather than prescribe what organisations should do.

The General Electric (GE) Business Screen

The GE Business Screen is another method of evaluating businesses along two dimensions:
* industry attractiveness
* competitive position.

Industry attractiveness and competitive position are used to classify businesses as winners, question marks, average businesses, losers or profit producers. The GE Business Screen suggests that several factors combine to determine a business's competitive position and the attractiveness of its industry (see Figure 9.2).

Figure 9.2 The General Electric (GE) Business Screen

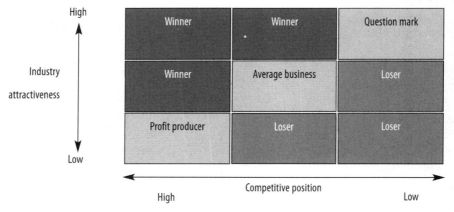

Source: Hofer and Schendel (1978)

Griffin (2008) suggests that **competitive position** is determined by:
• market share
• technological know-how
• product quality
• service network
• price competitiveness
• operating costs.

Griffin also suggests that **industry attractiveness** is determined by factors such as:
• market growth
• market size
• capital requirements
• competitive intensity.

According to the GE Business Screen, organisations should invest in winners and question marks, maintain the market position of average businesses and profit producers, and sell losers.

9.5 Strategic human resource management

Strategic human resource management focuses on the link or *vertical integration* between human resource practices and an organisation's business strategy in order to enhance performance. Vertical integration can be demonstrated through the linking of a business goal to individual objective setting and to the measurement and rewarding of that business goal. It also focuses on the relationship between best-practice or high-commitment human resource practices and organisational performance. The contribution that human resources may make to an organisation's performance and effectiveness has been linked to changes in the business environment, with the impact of globalisation leading to the need for increased competitiveness, flexibility, responsiveness, quality and the necessity for all functions of the business to demonstrate their contribution to the bottom line.

According to Beer *et al.* (1984), an organisation needs to establish a 'close fit' between its external business strategy and the elements of its internal human resource strategy. Similarly, Guest (1987) suggests that if the human resources component is not an integral part of the strategic planning process, the implementations of strategic business plans become more problematic. Because they are the most variable, and the least easy to understand and control of all management resources, effective utilisation of human resources is likely to give organisations a significant competitive advantage.

The human resource dimension must therefore be fully integrated into the strategic planning process. In order for organisations to gain a *competitive advantage* through their employees, human resource management must not be viewed as a standalone corporate issue but must be integrated with corporate strategy. Appropriate human resources are needed to implement strategies for an organisation to gain a competitive advantage through its human resources. Organisations, realising that their other resources may be easily imitated by competitors, might rely on their particular culture or team-working situation, which may be more difficult to imitate, in order to gain competitive advantage.

According to Bratton and Gold (2003), an alignment between business strategy and human resource management strategy will improve organisational performance and competitiveness. They suggest that improved organisational performance results from policies of empowerment, team working, workplace learning and employee commitment. Commitment to organisational competitiveness, as well as benefiting an organisation, also benefits employees by enhancing their perceptions of their own dignity, self-worth and identity. Guest *et al.* (1997) suggest that innovation is a necessary part of any effective strategy for organisational success. Herriot and Pemberton (1997) note that a number of human requirements are needed for the successful pursuit of a strategy of innovation, including:

- access to adequate resources
- security
- autonomy (individuals being able to make decisions about how their work gets done)
- team-working.

Overall, therefore, strategic human resource management is differentiated from human resource management in a number of ways, particularly in its movement away from a micro-perspective on individual human resource functional areas to the adoption of a macro-perspective with its subsequent emphasis on vertical integration. It becomes apparent that the meaning of strategic human resource management tends to lie in the context of organisational performance, although organisational performance can be interpreted and measured in a variety of ways. These may range from delivering efficiency and flexibility through cost reduction-driven strategies, to delivering employee commitment to organisational goals, to viewing human resources as a source of human capital and sustainable competitive advantage and a core business competence and key strategic asset. Employees are an important resource in the construction industry, with many skilled and unskilled workers being involved in the completion of a construction project. Integrating human resource management policies with the strategic objectives of a company should, therefore, improve overall organisational performance and project performance.

9.6 Key points

Strategy is a comprehensive plan for accomplishing an organisation's mission. *Strategic management* is a comprehensive and ongoing process aimed at formulating and implementing effective strategies. Many large organisations have corporate-level, business-level and functional-level strategies. A corporate-level strategy is a plan used by an organisation to manage its operations across several businesses. A business-level strategy is the plan an organisation uses to conduct its business.

Porter suggests that organisations may formulate a differentiation strategy, a cost-leadership strategy or a focus strategy at the business level. Miles and Snow suggest that, at the business level, organisations may choose from a defender strategy, a prospector strategy, an analyser strategy or a reactor strategy.

A functional-level strategy is the plan an organisation uses to manage its major operating departments in order to support corporate- and business-level strategies. An organisation may decide to operate in a number of different, unrelated businesses.

Organisations manage various businesses through *portfolio management techniques*.

- The BCG matrix classifies an organisation's various businesses as 'dogs, cash cows, question marks or stars', according to market share and market growth rate.
- The GE Business Screen classifies businesses as 'winners, losers, question marks, average businesses or profit producers', according to industry attractiveness and competitive position.

A further aspect of strategic management is concerned with the matching of internal and external demands for human resources, and with integrating the management of human resources in overall organisational planning. Effective human resource management is of vital strategic importance to an organisation and contributes to an organisation's competitive advantage over competitors.

Important terms and concepts

timber-framed house building (p. 148)
vertical integration (p. 156)

Questions for review

1. Outline the steps involved in the strategic management process.
2. Conduct an internal and external environmental analysis for a building company.
3. Differentiate between corporate, business and functional levels of strategy.
4. Explain how grand strategy options might apply to a national house building contractor.
5. Discuss how a pre-cast concrete products manufacturer could use a corporate portfolio approach in managing its business
6. Explain how employees can contribute to a company achieving a competitive advantage over its competitors.
7. Write brief notes on:
   a. strategic management
   b. Miles and Snow's business strategies
   c. strategic human resource management.

10

CURRENT MANAGEMENT ISSUES IN THE BUILT ENVIRONMENT

Learning outcomes

Following study of this chapter you will be able to:

- understand the extent of the decline in the construction sector
- understand the background and operation of the government's Capital Works Management Framework in the management of public capital projects
- understand the role of ethics and social responsibility for organisations in the built environment
- appreciate the roles of and barriers to women's participation in the construction sector
- recognise the contribution of diversity in the workplace
- understand the approach and rationale taken by CRH in managing its business during an economic downturn.

10.1 Introduction

While management ideas and techniques come into and go out of fashion, interest in management theory and practice in the built environment has increased in recent years as new issues and challenges have emerged. From a very wide range of issues that could be examined under the topic of current management issues in the built environment, this chapter includes the following important challenges facing managers in the built environment in the twenty-first century:

- decline in Ireland's construction industry
- reform of the management of capital works projects in the public sector
- ethics and social responsibility
- women in the construction sector
- workplace diversity
- managing in an economic downturn (see the CRH case study, page 175).

10.2 The decline in Ireland's construction industry

The built environment in Ireland has experienced a severe decline since its peak in 2007. Economic and industry forecasters have predicted that the industry will face major challenges in the next five to seven years (DKM 2009). The overall decline in construction activity in Ireland between 2007 and 2009 was -32 per cent, which represents a reduction in output of almost one third.

Figure 10.1 Decline in Ireland's construction activity

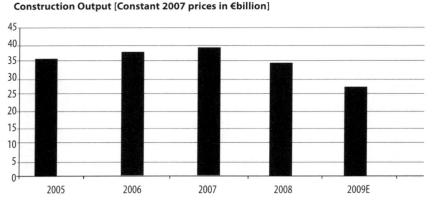

Construction Output [Constant 2007 prices in €billion]

Source: based on data from DKM (2009)

Employment in the construction sector

Employment in the construction industry is measured by the Central Statistics Office (CSO) as either direct or indirect labour. Directly employed persons are regarded as the people employed by construction companies. Indirectly employed persons, often called the 'second generation', are people in support industries such as materials suppliers, together with professional services employees such as architects, engineers and quantity surveyors. Figure 10.2 illustrates the trend in construction employment from 2005 to 2009. Overall, total construction employment fell by 28 per cent in 2009 and this was substantially caused by the reduction in house-building activity.

Certain sectors of the construction industry are more labour-intensive than others; for example, house building is more labour-intensive than civil engineering construction, which is plant- and equipment-intensive. The effects of decline in output, therefore, are noticeably different in different sub-sectors of construction.

Between 2007 and 2009, 121,000 employees directly or indirectly employed in the construction industry lost their jobs. In human resource management terms, the construction industry needs to be governed far more carefully to stabilise the workforce numbers at a more sustainable level in the future. For those people who will be unable to return to the construction industry, retraining and career change can be assisted by employers as part of a settlement and outsourcing service.

Figure 10.2 Decline in total employment in construction

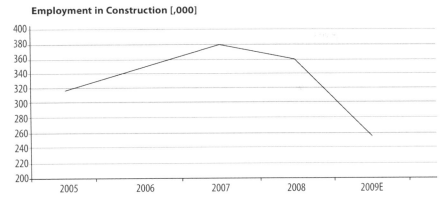

Source: based on data from DKM (2009)

10.3 Reform of the management of capital works projects in the public sector

Introduction to the Capital Works Management Framework

During the early years of the new millennium the Irish economy was thriving and medium-term predictions were for strong growth. The government at the time was implementing major capital development programmes to redress structural deficits in the provision of:

- hospitals
- schools
- public buildings
- roads
- water services
- telecommunications infrastructures (e.g. broadband).

Capital funding was available to finance these developments and the construction industry was eager to deliver them. Practices in the design and construction of these large-scale projects were not, however, yielding the results expected of them by government. Cost certainty on projects was poor, and there were frequent and substantial cost over-runs. Efficiency in the delivery of projects was reduced by frequent delays and excessive redesign of projects during the construction phase. It was clear that changes to existing practices were necessary, and these changes needed to be radical and to be backed by the full authority of government in order to be implemented successfully.

In 2006, the government implemented fundamental changes to the management of public projects and a new system known as the Capital Works

Management Framework (CWMF) was introduced. The strategic objectives of the CWMF are to ensure:

- greater cost certainty at contract award stage
- better value for money at all stages during project delivery, particularly at handover stage
- more efficient end-user delivery.

The management framework contains a compendium of best practice guidance, standard contracts and generic template documents that form four pillars which support the framework (see Table 10.1).

Table 10.1 The Capital Works Management Framework

Pillar 1	Pillar 2	Pillar 3	Pillar 4
A suite of standard forms of construction contracts and associated model forms, dispute resolution rules, model invitations to tender, forms of tender and schedules.	The standard conditions of engagement for consultants, dispute resolution rules, model invitations to tender, forms of tender and schedules.	Standard templates to record cost planning and control information; and for suitability assessment.	Extensive guidance notes covering the various management activities in the project delivery process.

Source: www.constructionprocurement.gov.ie

The Department of Finance is responsible for implementing national policy on public procurement, particularly in relation to construction procurement. The department's website, www.constructionprocurement.gov.ie, has been developed specifically to implement the key outputs of the government's decision in relation to the reform of public sector construction procurement.

Managing value and complexity

The CWMF has brought clarity and practical guidance to the management of value and complexity by establishing a value/complexity matrix (see Figure 10.3).

The value/complexity matrix indicates the appropriate level of management techniques that should be employed according to the category of a project in a particular sector of the industry. (See Chapter 2 for a breakdown of construction markets/sectors.) Each sector client can use his/her judgment to place their project into an appropriate category for the design team and contractor to manage. There are four categories:

- category 1—low-value, low-complexity projects
- category 2—low-value, high-complexity projects

Figure 10.3 Value/complexity matrix

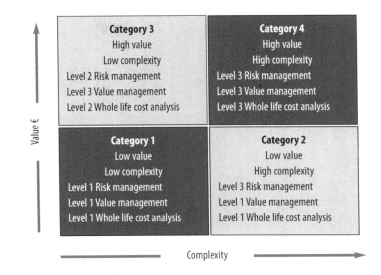

Source: www.constructionprocurement.gov.ie

- category 3—high-value, low-complexity projects
- category 4—high-value, high-complexity projects.

The key feature is the need for all projects to be assessed against the three management techniques of:
- risk
- value
- whole life cost analysis (i.e. the assessment of the costs associated with a building throughout its life span).

The framework gives technical guidance regarding the techniques to be employed for each level of risk management, value management and whole life cost analysis. Two examples below illustrate the effectiveness of the value/complexity matrix.

Example 1: High-value, high-complexity project

An example might be a new €100 million hospital. This type of project represents a high-value project for the health sector. A hospital requires very complex design, a high degree of functionality (the nature of the activities carried out within the facility) and a high degree of difficulty in construction. It should, therefore, be placed in category 4 project type and should have the highest (level 3) techniques of risk management, value management and whole life cost analysis applied to it.

Example 2: Low-value, high-complexity project

For example, a new fifty-metre underground water main to be constructed across an existing motorway, costing €100,000. In terms of water services projects it rates as a low-value project; however, the nature of the work is highly complex as the water main is to be constructed across an existing motorway. If the motorway is to be kept operational and the works to be carried out will use such techniques as directional drilling, the risks of disruption to traffic and accidental damage to other services under the motorway are high. This project would therefore be rated as a category 2 project, and the highest level of risk management techniques are required but the minimum level of value management and whole life cost analysis are appropriate.

The inclusion of the value/complexity matrix in the Capital Works Management Framework has enabled public clients in each of the construction sectors to apply appropriate levels of best management practice to their projects in compliance with the government's objectives of cost certainty, value for money and efficiency of project delivery.

10.4 Ethics and social responsibility

Ethics

The study of ethics is not new. Since the nineteenth century the need for ethical principles has been highlighted by social reformers. Current management literature on ethics, along with the topic of ethics in general, is a growing field of research. The study of ethics centres on choices facing individuals, and managerial ethics has been defined as the standards of behaviour that guide individual managers in their work (Donaldson and Dunfee 1994). Managerial ethics, therefore, is concerned with:

- norms
- values
- rights and responsibilities
- fairness
- being part of an organisation that establishes and maintains a set of moral rules.

Every organisation operates an ethical code based on codes of conduct embedded in company culture and expressed in the actions and decisions of senior management. One important area of managerial ethics is the way in which an organisation treats its employees. This includes working conditions, wages, hiring, and employee privacy and respect. An organisation's ethical code will be influenced by the societal norms, values and culture in which it operates. Ethics may be viewed as a subset of culture and where cultural differences exist, for example between different countries, different ethical standards are likely to prevail.

Another important area of managerial ethics is how employees treat the organisation. Examples of ethical issues for individual employees include:

- honesty
- confidentiality
- the divulging of organisational secrets (for example, by employees in a construction company who may be tempted to tell competitors of their employer's prices and tendering strategies).

Johns (1995) highlights examples of unethical behaviour, which applies not only to managerial staff but is also evident in the actions of non-managerial staff. These include:

- giving gifts or gratuities to buyers in the hope of influencing them
- dishonesty towards customers and clients
- theft of employer's property and materials
- reading other people's mail for personal advantage.

Senior management has the responsibility to enhance ethical behaviour as it establishes an organisation's culture and defines what will and will not be acceptable behaviour (Griffin 2008).

Managing social responsibility and ethics

Any philosophy or course of action that runs counter to public interest is not tolerated by society today (Hartley 1993). Organisations now face more critical scrutiny from stakeholders and operate in settings that are subject to an increasing number of regulations. As organisations, of necessity, interact with the environment in which they operate, they are regarded as having responsibilities to society.

Mason (2009) has identified the growing importance of ethical behaviour in the built environment, in particular a recent trend in the promotion of ethical values by contractors. Reasons for promoting ethical standards in the built environment include:

- growing awareness by the general public of environmental issues and climate change
- national and international agreements and protocols on environmental sustainability, for example, the Kyoto Protocol and the Copenhagen agreement
- improved enforcement by the EU and various agencies such as the Environmental Protection Agency (EPA) and the European Office of Fair Trade
- commercial benefits to construction companies of offering services and building processes that can be clearly labelled as complying with ethical and socially responsible standards.

Social responsibility has been defined as a set of obligations an organisation has to protect and enhance the society in which it functions (Griffin 2008). Organisations have many areas of social responsibility, including:

• the natural environment and built environment
• product responsibility
• promotional activities
• organisational stakeholders.

Social responsibility towards the natural and built environment has grown substantially during the past three decades. Protection of the natural environment is now a crucial worldwide issue facing organisations and the public. Environmentalists often view the construction industry as a destroyer of the natural environment through its activities in creating a built environment. The evolution of sustainable development and environmentally sensitive design, however, can allow for the construction and maintenance of a built environment in a manner that is sympathetic to the two environments.

The increasing awareness of the environment draws attention to some negative aspects of global industry:

• the disposal of hazardous waste (chemical, biological, medical and nuclear)
• the contamination of oceans and its impact on marine life
• air pollution, in particular the incidence of PCBs (polychlorinated biphenyls) and greenhouse gases such as carbon dioxide.

International conventions on climate change, such as the Kyoto Protocol (1997) and the Copenhagen agreement (2009) provide for a global approach to the management of environmental threats. These conventions lay down limits on pollution and market mechanisms to support developing countries to adopt cleaner technologies in running their economies.

The built environment sector has a significant role to play in improving the design standards of future buildings and reducing the negative environmental impacts of existing buildings. This has been reflected in Ireland's building regulations, which now require higher standards of energy performance and sustainability.

10.5 Women in the construction sector

One of the most significant features of the global labour market in the second half of the twentieth century was the increasing labour-force participation rate by women. EU statistics indicate that women make up 41 per cent of the working population. Throughout EU countries, however, job segregation based on gender still exists and over half of the female workforce is employed in the service sector, which includes trade, education, retail, health care and clerical duties.

Women in corporate environments tend to be at the lower end of managerial hierarchies, even after a decade or more in management jobs, and fewer than 5 per cent hold *senior* management positions. Overall, research shows that women employed in EU countries do not enjoy the same job conditions, pay, status and career opportunities as their male counterparts (Davidson and Cooper 1992; Linehan 2000). According to the Central Statistics Office's Census of Population (2006), female employees in the building and construction industry in Ireland in 2006 accounted for just 2.5 per cent of the total workforce.

In a number of countries, while women are gaining managerial experience, they still encounter a **glass ceiling**—a term used to describe 'a barrier so subtle that it is transparent, yet so strong that it prevents women and minorities from moving up the managerial hierarchy' (Morrison and Von Glinow 1990). There are major organisational barriers contributing to the glass ceiling, including:

- a lonely and non-supportive working environment
- the treatment of differences as weaknesses
- the exclusion of people from group activities because of their differences
- the difficulty of balancing work and family life (in construction, this is a particular problem for women in older age groups, part-time and flexible working women).

There is now extensive evidence, from Australia, North America and Europe, that indicates that women face far more career-development obstacles than their male counterparts. The specific problems and pressures that have been identified as unique to women managers include:

- being a test case for future women
- the lack of role models
- feelings of isolation
- the strains of coping with prejudice and sex stereotyping
- overt and indirect discrimination by fellow employees and employers, as well as from organisational structures and cultures.

For a number of years women have been moving into professional work such as law, accountancy and medicine, all of which require high-level qualifications and are considered attractive because of their perceived high level of social status. Today, there are almost equal numbers of women and men in these sectors. Occupational sectors such as engineering and construction, however, have not seen a corresponding change in the make-up of the workforce.

Almost all cultures differentiate between male and female roles (Adler 1987). Societies expect women to behave differently from men. Many of the constraints that tend to prevent women from attaining senior managerial positions are quite similar in most countries. There are, for example, cultural, educational, legislative, attitudinal and corporate constraints in most countries. The depth of each constraint varies from society to society.

Covert barriers that women in management have to overcome include:

- a scarcity of mentors (persons in an organisation who provide training, advice,

    direction and support for a more junior person)
- being a member of a minority group in organisations
- a lack of networking

—all of which hinder women managers in their progression to senior managerial positions (Linehan 2000).

Peer relationships and interpersonal networks provide a source of organisational support, but women have been largely excluded from 'old boy networks' which traditionally are composed of individuals who hold power in organisations. The Construction Industry Federation in Ireland set up a business network for women in construction which aims to promote and support the advancement of women in construction through its regional networks. Using the collective strength of the networks it offers a forum for its members, who are involved in all sectors of the construction industry, to exchange ideas, information and skills. The Construction Business Network for Women was established in 1997 and was the result of an EU-funded project to develop a programme for women involved in strategic management of construction companies. The current membership consists of owner managers and senior management staff from all sectors of the construction industry. There is also an international association for women in construction, the National Association for Women in Construction (NAWIC) which was founded in the United States fifty years ago. It was originally set up as a type of support group for women in the construction industry and now has over six thousand members worldwide. In March 2009, NAWIC Ireland was launched to offer professionals in the construction industry the opportunity to access information and develop business with other people working in this sector. One of the main advantages for the members of NAWIC is that they can create links with professionals in the sector in many countries.

Research in Europe (Linehan 2000) suggests that women managers engage less in career planning than their male counterparts because they are often discriminated against by organisational career policies. Women managers perceive that male managers still select, recruit and promote people who most resemble themselves; therefore, for women, gender is generally considered to be a disadvantage for job promotion or career prospects. As top managers are likely to have the major impact on the scope and pattern of women's career development, a positive attitude from managers to equality can promote the career development of more women, while a negative attitude can militate against women advancing beyond lower management levels (Rothwell 1984). Much depends on an organisation's view of women; that is, whether they are seen primarily as an investment or an expense (Storey 1989).

Research findings also establish that male attitudes to managerial women are strong, consistent and pervasive, and appear to be a global phenomenon (Schein et al. 1994). Research also predicts that the progression of women to senior management positions will be kept low if the attitudes of male decision-makers, who are influenced strongly by managerial sex typing, are allowed to go unchecked (Schein 1994).

Additionally, the long hours and the need to be office-based prove difficult for female employees with children, making work–life balance a serious barrier to retaining women in the construction industry. According to research carried out by the Chartered Institute of Building (CIOB), construction companies will have to implement creative solutions, such as re-training to update skills, flexi-time and part-time working hours, working from home and job sharing in order to recruit and keep female employees at all levels of construction work.

As in all industries, the construction sector needs diversity to sustain development. The industry needs to attract women when they are choosing a career path. Construction and engineering are still very male-dominated professions, with 90 per cent of learners being men, while hairdressing and beauty therapy are dominated by women, who make up 91 per cent of learners (CIOB 2008). Table 10.2 shows the figures for full-time undergraduate students entering construction-related courses in 2008/09.

Table 10.2 Full-time undergraduate students entering construction-related courses in 2008/09

Gender	Universities		Institutes of Technology		Total (All Sectors)	
	No.	%	No.	%	No.	%
Male	668	74	1,959	90	2,627	85
Female	231	26	226	10	457	15
Total	899	100	2,185	100	3,084	100

Source: www.hea.ie

Research in the UK that focused on the experiences of female engineers working on construction sites identified that the UK construction industry has traditionally been, and still is, largely dominated by white male workers (Bagilhole et al. 2002). The research also found that in order for the construction industry to attract and retain women it requires a more comprehensive understanding of women's career experiences and subsequently recommended that human resource management practices should be developed to enable women to progress their careers in the construction sector.

Greenhaus and Callanan (1994) conclude that there are very good reasons for encouraging gender balance in traditionally male-dominated industries: for example, gender balance leads to more broadly informed, adaptable organisations, which are more understanding of their customers, more responsive to change and better able to attract higher-calibre employees.

10.6 Workplace diversity

Workforce diversity is an issue which poses numerous challenges for managers. The term 'diversity' is often used broadly to refer to many variables, including, but not limited to:

- race
- gender
- religion
- colour
- national origin
- disability
- sexual orientation
- age
- education
- geographic origin
- skill characteristics.

Diversity differs from discrimination, because diversity is about variety and differences while discrimination concerns treating people differently because of prejudice.

In 2006, research into human resource management, partnership, diversity and equality in Ireland was conducted on behalf of the National Centre for Partnership and Performance (NCPP) and the Equality Authority (EA). The findings on diversity among manufacturing companies, which included firms in the built environment, identified that high-performance companies with higher levels of labour productivity and workforce innovation, and lower levels of employee turnover, are managing their organisations in ways that are distinctly different from average-performing companies. One of the key features of these high-performance companies was their use of formal polices and practices in the recruitment, training and staff development in the creation of a diverse workforce (NCPP and EA 2008)

Many organisations, including construction companies, have found that diversity can be a source of competitive advantage in the marketplace (NCPP and EA 2008). Organisations that manage diversity effectively become known among minorities as good places to work, and in turn, these organisations will generally have lower levels of turnover and absenteeism. By discriminating on the basis of gender, race, ethnicity or disability, managers run the risk of neglecting or overlooking talented employees. The consequence is that the organisation fails to maximise its full human resource potential and valuable resources are wasted through under-utilising the competence of existing employees or losing talented staff to other organisations.

10.7 Key points

This chapter focused on current management issues facing the construction industry in Ireland. There has been a large decline in Ireland's construction industry in recent years, leading to a current high rate of unemployment in the industry. Many people are up-skilling or making a career change in order to return to work.

The reform of the *management of capital works projects* in the public sector has led to best practice being implemented on public sector projects, with a greater emphasis on cost certainty, value for money and efficiency of project delivery.

Ethics involves personal beliefs about what constitutes right and wrong behaviour. The ethical context of an organisation is founded on the shared values of its individual managers and on the dominant messages arising from organisational practices. Social responsibility is the set of obligations an organisation has to protect and enhance the society in which it functions.

Women in the construction sector face more career obstacles, and overt and covert barriers to their career progression, than their male counterparts. Organisations cannot, however, afford to ignore the increasing presence of women in the construction industry. Broadening an organisation's management pool, including and promoting women in domestic economies as well as internationally, should help to achieve competitive advantage for the organisation.

The workforce in organisations today is becoming increasingly diverse, a development that affects employees' lives and poses numerous challenges to managers. Managers need to create diversity awareness, and to appreciate the numerous positive benefits of a diverse workforce.

Important terms and concepts

Capital Works Management Framework (p. 163)
decline in construction activity (p. 161)
employment in construction (p. 162)
ethics (p. 166)
glass ceiling (p. 169)
social responsibility (p. 167)
value/complexity matrix (p. 164)
women in the construction sector (p. 168)
workplace diversity (p. 172)

Questions for review

1. Describe the extent of the decline in the construction sector from 2005 to 2009 in terms of:
    a. construction activity
    b. construction employment.
2. Outline the changes to the management of public capital works required by the government.
3. Examine the implications of ethics and social responsibility in the management of contemporary organisations in the built environment.
4. Identity some of the barriers to women in the construction industry and suggest how these barriers may be overcome.
5. Explain the nature of workforce diversity.

CRH case study: Managing business in an economic downturn

Introduction

CRH plc is an international group of companies engaged in the manufacture and supply of a wide range of building materials. With its headquarters in Dublin, CRH is the largest company quoted on the Irish Stock Exchange and employs approximately 80,000 people worldwide.

CRH operates in cyclical industries that are affected by factors beyond its control, such as the level of construction activity, fuel and raw material prices. These factors are in turn affected by the performance of national markets and the global economy.

CRH has taken steps to deal with the current economic downturn and to position its business to take advantage of opportunities when the world's economies begin to recover.

Performance and growth

In the industry sector in which it operates, CRH is a responsible leader, delivering consistent performance and growth. In 1970 approximately 95 per cent of CRH's activities were in Ireland. However, by 2008 only 8 per cent of the group's business was conducted in Ireland. CRH realised that as an indigenous company in a small open economy its potential growth would be limited. Management determined that it needed to expand and grow by both re-investing in its existing businesses and selectively buying other companies in new markets. This latter approach is called diversification.

Managing a well-balanced portfolio of products is key to easing the impact of the economic downturn on business. The group focuses on three core business segments: materials, products and distribution.

- **Primary materials**—businesses involved in the production of cement, aggregates, asphalt, concrete and ready-mixed concrete to construct the building frame.
- **Value-added building products**—businesses involved in the production of concrete products and a range of other construction-related products and services to complete the building envelope.
- **Specialist building materials distribution**—businesses engaged in the marketing and sale of builders' supplies to the construction industry and of materials and products to DIY (do it yourself) customers.

Since the mid-1970s, the group has expanded through inorganic growth (acquisition—acquiring/buying firms) and organic growth (developing existing businesses, financed by the reserves of the company) into an international manufacturer and supplier of building materials. CRH now has operations in thirty-five countries, mainly in Western Europe and North America and in developing markets in Eastern Europe, South America, Turkey, China and India.

What is a recession?

A recession is a general slowdown in economic activity over a sustained period of time. During a recession, production, as measured by gross domestic product (GDP), employment, investment spending, household incomes and business profits, falls.

Survival during a recession

Surviving a recession is a major challenge for any company. It is crucial for businesses to make whatever changes are necessary to their operations to ensure that they can continue to remain viable at lower levels of commercial activity.

CRH's unique regional and product balance reduces the potential effects of industry and economic cycles:

- **Regional diversification** involves establishing businesses to achieve leadership positions across countries. This has been practised by CRH since the 1970s. The likelihood of all the markets collapsing at the same time becomes lower and lower when a strong presence is developed in more and more markets.
- **Product diversification** involves broadening the range of products and services offered to customers in different sectors of the construction industry.

Managing operations

CRH's success as a global business depends, in part, upon its ability to succeed in fast-changing economic conditions. CRH is a decentralised group with many subsidiary companies operating under a wide range of local and regional brand/trade names.

CRH's strategy has been to build leadership positions in regional and local markets. By delegating authority to local managers, decisions can be made promptly by those most familiar with local economic conditions, while central support from CRH Group ensures that sustainable growth is achieved in line with the group's strategic goals. Central functions include the board, which sets the strategic direction for the group, and human resources, finance and IT, which support the implementation of day-to-day management policy. As a result, CRH's vision can be described as focusing globally yet managing locally.

During a recession, it is important for businesses to look for new ways to maximise performance. One such way is to improve efficiency across operations. Another way is to reinvest capital through the use of retained earnings/revenue reserves in its existing facilities. This helps to improve energy and operational efficiency and to match capacity to meet current and future demand.

Managing suppliers

Individual operating companies source raw materials in the region in which they operate. Most of these suppliers are based in Europe or North America. Deteriorating demand in these markets requires strict expenditure controls. Management's current focus is on sourcing quality supplies to achieve cost reductions and to increase efficiency. Central sourcing functions have been established in key markets to take advantage of economies of scale and reduce the cost of purchased goods.

Managing finances

Recession strategies

The recent banking crisis has made it more difficult for companies to obtain financing. Monitoring the business by maintaining liquidity and adequate cash flow is crucial. However, current market conditions have made it more expensive to obtain financing for operations, hence increasing the costs of running a business. Like many companies, CRH is focusing on maximising cash flow from operations and reducing working capital.

Budgeting—cost savings

The year 2008 saw major changes in the financial, economic and business climate worldwide. Declining markets led to wide-ranging cutbacks across CRH's businesses. The company also slowed its rate of acquisition and its capital expenditure to improve liquidity and take advantage of possible further reductions in the price of assets. CRH management also implemented several energy- and cost-reduction initiatives in 2008 and 2009 to limit the decline in profit.

Division-wide procurement strategies and purchasing programmes contributed to reducing the cost of purchased materials and supplies by availing of economies of scale. Operational excellence initiatives have helped to reduce both labour and equipment costs while eliminating waste. Reductions in fixed overhead staffing and other fixed costs have been progressively implemented to maintain a strong balance sheet position.

Raising capital—sources of finance

In early 2009, CRH management undertook a successful rights issue. This allowed existing ordinary shareholders to buy more shares as a way of re-investing back into the business. The funds raised are for further acquisitions as potential assets come on to the market from more troubled industry players.

In 2009, despite the very challenging trading backdrop, CRH is operating a healthy cash flow. The group continues to identify new measures to deal with the evolving trading conditions. CRH believes that its current cash flows, together with the recent rights issue and funds raised through its borrowing facilities, are more than sufficient to meet its expenditure requirements for the foreseeable future.

Financial reporting

In a group such as CRH it is essential that IT systems give prompt, consistent and reliable financial reporting from the local operating units to the central group management. Accurate financial reporting is crucial for management, particularly during difficult economic circumstances. Decisions on budgeting, raising capital and sourcing finance all rely on accurate financial reporting.

Managing people

CRH employs 80,000 people in more than 3,700 locations, spanning thirty-five countries. These people are managed through four divisions. This year the company is launching a web-based global talent management system, which will replace a paper-based system.

There is a unique culture of performance and achievement throughout the group, ensuring that, even in the current exceptionally difficult economic environment, CRH has the capacity to deliver performance excellence.

The CRH management team are highly experienced and the development of talented successors is a priority for all managers. Regular formal reviews of management development strategy are carried out by each division, with guidance and support provided by the group human resources function.

Typically, CRH managers come from three very different streams:
- internally developed operating managers who have room to grow in an expanding organisation
- highly qualified finance and development professionals—business builders with vision and future potential
- owner-entrepreneurs who have joined with their companies and provide a vibrant entrepreneurial spirit.

This results in a healthy mix and depth of skills and a wealth of experience at senior level with many senior leaders having managed through previous economic cycles. This gives them invaluable experience to deal with the current downturn, enabling them to prepare for the inevitable upturn of the market.

Performance management

Achieving results is a critical aspect of CRH's high-performance culture, particularly during difficult economic times. CRH has adopted a strong performance management and appraisal process. Employees are set realistic goals and plans are put in place to achieve them. Performance is driven by appraisal, regular review meetings and self-assessment.

Leadership development

Management development programmes provide leadership training, usually to middle or top-level managers, to assist them in upgrading their skills. The programmes have been updated in response to the changing economic climate. Employees are encouraged to identify opportunities for business development and increased efficiency. Internal promotion is a key source of leadership talent and is used to motivate and reward staff.

Succession planning

CRH places a significant emphasis on succession planning. This is done to develop future generations of leaders from within the organisation and to maintain quality employees at all levels. Preparing people for future roles involves a combination of challenging assignments, coaching and formal training.

Employees are aware that during difficult economic times they must work under tighter financial constraints to keep operations within budget.

Managing the future

The overall outlook is extremely challenging, given the severe impact of ongoing turmoil in financial markets across the world. There are a number of positive aspects which will provide future opportunities for business, for example lower energy costs, interest rate reductions and the infrastructure stimulus packages in a number of countries, notably the USA. In this environment, efforts will remain focused on implementing cost-cutting measures, reducing expenditure and preparing the business for recovery in construction markets.

Regional and product diversity serve to smooth out some of the effects of changing economic conditions and to provide multiple opportunities for growth. Management has responded vigorously to extremely challenging market conditions. All aspects of business have been analysed, and cost reduction and cash generation measures have been put in place to deal with whatever trading circumstances may evolve.

Glossary

Acquisition:	The act of acquiring something, in this context buying businesses as assets, i.e. a form of inorganic growth.
Assets:	The total resources of a person or business, which includes cash, stock, inventory, accounts receivable, goodwill, fixtures, machinery, real estate, etc.
Balance sheet:	A financial statement showing a company's assets, liabilities and shareholders' equity on a given date. It shows what the company owns and what debts it owes.
Decentralisation:	When power and authority is delegated throughout the

Diversification:
organisation rather than being vested in the hands of a few senior managers.

Diversification:
The broadening of business activities to expand into other countries and/or products to add complementary products and services.

Economies of scale:
This occurs when more of a good or service is produced: the cost of producing each unit of that good or service is reduced.

Inorganic growth:
When a firm acquires other companies, merges with other firms or forms alliances.

Organic growth:
Developing existing businesses financed from the reserves of the company.

Rights issue:
A rights issue is a way in which a company can raise money by selling new shares. These newly issued shares are offered to existing shareholders in proportion to their current shareholding at a discount from the price at which they will be offered to the public later.

Source: *http://www.business2000.ie*. Reproduced with kind permission of CRH and Business 2000.

Questions for review

1. Explain what is meant by the term 'small open economy'. Briefly outline how CRH continues to grow despite limited market size in Ireland.
2. Distinguish between organic and inorganic growth.
3. Outline the factors that are beyond the control of CRH and that affect its growth.
4. Explain the term 'decentralised management structure'.
5. Analyse the challenges facing CRH as a result of difficult current market conditions.
6. Evaluate how CRH has responded to the current economic downturn.
7. 'CRH has adopted a strong performance management and appraisal process.' Outline the key elements of this process.
8. Evaluate the arguments in favour of or against CRH further expanding its operations in the current economic climate.

REFERENCES

Adler, N.J. 1987. 'Pacific Basin Managers: A Gaijin, Not A Woman', *Human Resource Management*, 26(2), 169–92.

Advisory Conciliation and Arbitration Service (ACAS). 1982. *Workplace Communications*, Advisory Booklet no. 8. London: ACAS.

Aktouf, O. 1996. *Traditional Management and Beyond*. Montreal: Morin.

Alderfer, P. 1969. 'An Empirical Test of a New Theory of Human Needs', *Organisational Behaviour and Human Performance*, 4, 142–75.

Bagilhole B., A. Dainty and R. Neale. 2002. 'A Woman Engineer's Experiences of Working on British Construction Sites', *International Journal of Engineering*, 18 (4), 422–9.

Barham, K. and C. Rassam. 1989. *Shaping the Corporate Future*. London: Unwin Hyman.

Barney, J. 1996. 'Strategic Factor Markets', *Management Science*, December, 1231–41.

Beer, M., B. Spector and P.R. Lawrence. 1984. *Managing Human Assets*. New York: Free Press.

Berridge, J. and C. Cooper. 1994. 'The Employee Assistance Programme: Its Role in Organisational Coping and Excellence', *Personnel Review*, 23(7), 4–20.

Blake, R. and Mouton, J. 1962. 'The Managerial Grid', *Advanced Managerial Office Executive*, 1(9).

Bratton, J. and J. Gold. 2003. *Human Resource Management: Theory and Practice* (3rd edition). London: Macmillan.

Capowski. 1994. 'Anatomy of the Leader: Where are the Leaders of Tomorrow?' *Management Review*, March, 12.

Chartered Institute of Building. 1997. *The Code of Estimating Practice* (5th edition). Ascot: Chartered Institute of Building.

Chartered Institute of Building. 2008. *Skills Shortages in the UK Construction Industry*. Berkshire: Chartered Institute of Building.

Cooke, B and P. Williams. 1998. *Construction Planning, Programming and Control*. London: Macmillan.

Cooper, M. D. 1995. 'Motivation: Determining Influences on Behaviour', in T. Hannagan (ed.), *Management: Concepts and Practices*. London: Pitman.

Daft, R. 1998. *Organisation Theory and Design* (6th edition). Cincinnati, Ohio: South-Western.

Davidson, M.J. and C.L. Cooper. 1992. *Shattering the Glass Ceiling: The Woman Manager*. London: Paul Chapman.

DKM Economic Consultants. 2009. *Review of the Construction Industry 2008 and Outlook 2009–2011*. Dublin: DKM Economic Consultants.

Donaldson, T. and T.W. Dunfee. 1994. 'Toward a Unified Conception of Business Ethics: An Integrative Social Contracts Theory', *Academy of Management Review* 19(2), 252–84.

Drucker, P. 1954. *The Practice of Management*, London: Heinemann.

Eisenhardt, K.M., J.L. Kaahwajy and L.J. Bourgeois. 1997. 'How Management Teams Can Have a Good Fight', *Harvard Business Review*, July–August: 77–89.

Fayol, H. 1916. *Administration Industrielle et Générale* (1916), translated as *General and Industrial Management*. London: Pitman 1949.

Fryer, B. 1997. *The Practice of Construction Management*. Oxford: Blackwell Science.

Fryer, B. 2004. *The Practice of Construction Management* (5th edition). Oxford: Blackwell.

Greenhaus J. and G. Callanan. (1994), *Career Management* (2nd edition). Orlando: Dryden Press.

Griffin, R.W. 1999. *Management* (6th edition). New York: Houghton Mifflin.

Guest, D.E. 1987. 'Human Resource Management and Industrial Relations', *Journal of Management Studies,* 24(5), 503–21.

Guest, D., J. Storey and W. Tate. 1997. *Innovation: Opportunity through People*, consultative document. London: Institute of Personnel and Development.

Gunnigle, P., G. McMahon and G. Fitzgerald. 1999. *Industrial Relations in Ireland: Theory and Practice* (2nd edition). Dublin: Gill & Macmillan.

Gurjao, S. 2008. *The Changing Role of Women in the Construction Workforce*. Reading: Chartered Institute of Building.

Hague, D.J. 1985. 'Incentives and Motivation in the Construction Industry: A Critique', *Construction Management and Economics*, 3(2), 163–70.

Hannagan, T. 2008. *Management: Concepts and Practices* (5th edition). London: Financial Times Management.

Harris, F. and R. McCaffer. 2001. *Modern Construction Management*. Oxford: Blackwell.

Harrison, R. 2000. *Employee Development* (2nd edition). London: Institute of Personnel Management.

Hartley, R.F. 1993. *Business Ethics: Violations of the Public Trust*. New York: John Wiley.

Herriot, P. and C. Pemberton. 1997. 'Facilitating New Deals', *Human Resource Management Journal*, 7(1), 45–56.

Hofer, C. and D. Schendel. 1978. *Strategy Formulation: Analytical Concepts*. Ohio: West Publishing.

Johns, T. 1995. 'Don't Be Afraid of The Moral Maze', *People Management*, October: 32–4.

Kotter, J. 1986. *The General Managers*. New York: Free Press.

Langford, D., M.R. Hancock, R.Fellows and A.W. Gale. 1998. *Human Resource Management in Construction*. London: Longman.

Lavender, S. 1996. *Management for the Construction Industry*. Essex: Addison Wesley.

Lawrence, P.R. and J.W. Lorsch. 1967. *Organisation and Environment*. Boston:

Harvard University Press.

Legge, K. 1995. 'Human Resource Management: Rhetoric, Reality and Hidden Agendas', in J. Storey (ed.), *Human Resource Management: A Critical Text*. London: Routledge.

Linehan, M. 2000. *Senior Female International Managers: Why So Few?* Aldershot: Ashgate.

Locke, E. A. 1968. 'Toward a Theory of Task Motivation and Incentives', *Organisation Behaviour and Human Performance*, 3, 157–89.

March, C. 2009. *Business Organisation for Construction*. London: Taylor and Francis.

Marchington, M. and A. Wilkinson. 2000. *Core Personnel and Development* (2nd edition). London: Institute of Personnel and Development.

Mason, J. 2009. 'Delivering Ethical Improvement through Contractual Good Faith', in P. Fewings, *Ethics for the Built Environment*. New York: Taylor and Francis, pp. 281–91.

Miles, R.E. and C.C. Snow. 1984. *Organisational Strategy, Structure and Process*. New York: McGraw-Hill.

Mintzberg, H. 1973. *The Nature of Managerial Work*. New York: Harper & Row.

Mintzberg, H. 1979. *The Structuring of Organisations — A Synthesis of the Research*. Prentice Hall.

Morrison, A.M. and M.A. Von Glinow. 1990. 'Women and Minorities in Management', *American Psychologist*, 45(2), 200–8.

Mullins, L.J. 2007. *Management and Organizational Behaviour* (8th edition). London: Financial Times Pitman Publishing.

National Centre for Partnership and Performance (NCPP) and Equality Authority (EA). 2008. *New Models of High Performance Work Systems*. Dublin: NCPP and EA.

Naoum, S. 2001. *People and Organisational Management in Construction*. London: Thomas Telford.

Naylor, J. 2004. *Management* (2nd edition). London: Financial Times Pitman Publishing.

Needles, E., H.R. Anderson and J.C. Caldwell. 1999. *Principles of Accounting*. Boston: Houghton Mifflin.

Pearce, J.A. and F. David. 1987. 'Corporate Mission Statements: The Bottom Line', *Academy of Management Executive*, May, 109.

Peters, T.J. and R.H. Waterman. 1989. *In Search of Excellence: Lessons from America's Best-run Companies*. London: Harper & Row.

Pilcher, R. 1992. *Principles of Construction Management*. London: McGraw-Hill.

Porter, M. 1996. 'Competitive Strategy: Techniques for Analyzing Industries and Competitors', *Academy of Management Journal*, April, 255–91.

Porter, M. 1980. *Competitive Strategy: Techniques for Analysing Industries and Competitors*. New York: Free Press.

Quinn, F. 2002. *Crowning the Customer: How to Become Customer Driven.* Dublin: O'Brien Press.

Rothwell, S. 1984. 'Positive Action on Women's Career Development: An Overview of the Issues for Individuals and Organisations', in C.L. Cooper and M.J. Davidson (eds), *Women in Management: Career Development for Managerial Success.* London: Heinemann, pp. 3–31.

RTÉ 1998. *Primetime.* Quoted in the *Irish Times,* 4 February 1998, p. 3.

Schein, V.E. 1989. *Sex Role Stereotyping and Requisite Management Characteristics, Past, Present and Future,* Working paper series, no. WC 98–26, University of Western Ontario, National Centre for Management Research and Development.

Schein, V.E. 1994. 'Managerial Sex Typing: A Persistent and Pervasive Barrier to Women's Opportunities', in M.J. Davidson and R.J. Burke (eds), *Women in Management: Current Research Issues.* London: Paul Chapman, pp. 41–52.

Schein, V.E., R. Mueller, T. Lituchy and J. Liu. 1994. *Think Manager — Think Male: A Global Phenomenon?,* Gettysburg College Management Department Working Papers, Gettysburg, PA.

Senge, P.M. 1990. *The Fifth Discipline: The Art and Practice of the Learning Organisation.* New York: Doubleday.

Steers, R.M. and L.W. Porter. (eds). 1991. *Motivation and Work Behaviour* (5th edition). New York: McGraw-Hill.

Storey, J. (ed.) 1989. *New Perspectives on Human Resource Management.* London: Routledge.

Tannenbaum, R. and W.H. Schmidt. 1958. 'How to Choose a Leadership Pattern', *Harvard Business Review,* March/April.

Taylor, F.W. 1911. *Principles of Scientific Management.* New York: Harper & Brothers.

Turley, D. 1986. 'Some perspectives on the Irish consumer', *Irish Marketing Review,* 1.

Websites

BATU (Building and Allied Trades Union)	www.batu.ie
Business 2000	www.business2000.ie
CEF (Construction Employees Federation)	www.cefni.co.uk
Cement Roadstone Holdings	www.crh.ie
Chartered Institute of Building (CIOB)	www.ciob.ord.uk
Construction Industry Federation	www.cif.ie
Davis Langdon PKS	www.dlphs.ie
DKM Economic Consultants	www.dkm.ie
Dublin Bricklayers (Dublin branch of BATU)	www.dublinbricklayers.com
Engineers Ireland	www.iei.ie

Higher Education Authority (HEA)	www.hea.ie
Irish Auctioneers and Valuers Institute	www.iavi.ie
Kingspan	www.kingspan.ie
Michael Punch and Partners	www.mpp.ie
Public procurement website	www.constructionprocurement.ie
Roadstone	www.roadstone.ie
Royal Institute of Architects of Ireland	www.riai.ie
SIPTU	www.siptu.ie
Sisk Ltd	www.sisk.ie
Society of Chartered Surveyors	www.scs.ie
Union of Construction, Allied Trades and Technicans	www.ucatt.ie